March on the Dakota's:

The Sibley Expedition of 1863

Fern

Hope you enjoy the book.

Susan Kudelka

By: Susan Mary Kudelka

MARCH ON THE DAKOTA'S:
THE SIBLEY EXPEDITION OF 1863

Author - Susan Mary Kudelka
Publisher - McCleery & Sons Publishing
Photography - Susan Mary Kudelka
Dedication Copy - Susan Mary Kudelka & Scott Kudelka
About the Author Copy - Susan Mary Kudelka & Scott Kudelka

International Standard Book Number: 1-931916-22-5
Printed in the United States of America

I dedicate this book to my Grandfather Earl Frank Heath. Earl grew up on the wide open great plains of North Dakota and Montana. A successful farmer, Earl and his wife Mary raised four children along the Sheyenne River near Lisbon, North Dakota. In his free time Earl enjoyed exploring for archaeology artifacts, fishing for northerns, hunting white-tail deer, and the solitude of life along the river. During the 1930s Earl worked at a Civilian Conservation camp in Itasca State Park operating a saw mill and helping build park facilities. He enjoyed his work as a Federal Predator Control hunter and setting up electrical lines in rural areas of southeast North Dakota. For a number of years Earl owned Camp Hayes site, flying an American Flag to mark this historic spot. Earl passed away on December 17, 1997.

The 1862 Dakota Conflict

In August 1862, with the Civil War in its sixteenth month, relations between Minnesota settlers and the Santee Sioux reached the boiling point. Tricked into and betrayed by broken treaties, cheated incessantly by white traders, and brought to the brink of starvation by the government's delays in dispensing annuity payments, the Santee Sioux finally had enough.[1] The flash point, according to a persistent legend, was a confrontation between a settler and some Santee, whose manhood the settler had disparaged. The settler, his wife, and some of the settler's friends were killed.

Faced with almost certain reprisals, Little Crow, a respected Sioux leader, joined with his war chiefs and a week-long rampage began. Isolated settlers died by the hundreds—the Sioux took few prisoner. The nearby Army garrison and town of New Ulm were attacked. Even though outnumbered, the army prevailed, leaving many warriors dead and the rest disheartened. Little Crow, with a dwindling band, escaped to Canada, but the remaining Sioux were rounded up by the army, and hundreds, without benefit of defense counsel, were summarily sentenced to death by a military court. President Lincoln reduced the number of condemned, and 38 Sioux were duly hung, but the Dakota Conflict continued for decades as other tribes took up the fight.

The 1862 Dakota Conflict was caused by a number of factors, but the primary causes were white settlement and the failure of the United States government to honor commitments.

On July 23, 1851, the Wahpeton and Sisseton bands of the Upper Sioux ceded their lands in southern and western Minnesota Territory, Iowa, and Dakota. They were to be paid $1,665,000 in cash and annuities. A few days later on August 5, two bands of the Lower Sioux, the Mdewakanton and Wahpekute, signed away land in what is now southeast quarter of present day Minnesota. They were to be paid $1,410,000 in cash and annuities over a fifty-year period. Three years later, the former Indian land, almost 24,000,000 acres, was legally opened to white settlers. This left 7,000 Sioux in two small reservations, each twenty miles wide and seventy miles long, bordering the upper Minnesota River.[2]

The Upper Sioux found the assigned land favorable. The Lower Sioux, however, were not satisfied, because their reservation was prairie land and they favored woodlands. As well as resenting the location of the reservations, the Indians believed they had been cheated during the transactions. At Traverse des Sioux, they asserted that the whites had tricked them into signing a "traders paper," giving to traders and mixed-bloods, for claims against the Indians, some $400,000.00 which otherwise would have been paid to the tribes in cash. By 1857, white settlers had crowded close to the reservation boundaries and wanted further reduction of the Indians' territory. In 1858, the Sioux agreed to sell a strip of land along the north side of the Minnesota River, nearly a million acres, for a price fixed by the Senate. However, it was two years before congress appropriated thirty cents an acre in payment. The tribes deeply resented the insulting price.[3]

In 1857, a renegade band of Lower Sioux led by Inkpaduta (Scarlet Point or Red Plume) killed over thirty people in Iowa and several more later in Jackson County, Minnesota. Inkpaduta then escaped to Dakota Territory and out of desperation the Indian office at Washington notified the Minnesota Sioux that they would be held responsible for his apprehension. Until he was captured, no annuities would be paid. A short time later this requirement was dropped. The damage, however, had been done.[4]

In 1862, several factors came into play to encourage the Indians to act. One was that many of the young male settlers had left for southern battlefields, leaving the army's ranks depleted. Another was that a crop failure the previous fall had led to a state of near-starvation in the winter 1861-62. The third factor, and probably the most important, was the late arrival of the annuity goods and cash for the tribe. Congress was quibbling over whether to pay in paper currency or gold. The annuities had been expected by the Indians in June and did not arrive until August. The Indians' grievances increased when the promised food supplies did not arrive. One storekeeper, who refused to extend the Indians credit, said, "If they are hungry, let them eat grass or their own dung." Later, he was found dead, with his mouth stuffed with grass.[5]

Following the military action of 1862, the U. S. government began collecting an army at various posts and temporary stockades of the state, in preparation for a move northwestward to the Dakota Territories in the early summer of 1863. The campaign was organized by General John Pope, with the intent to subdue the Sioux. Two expeditions were planned, one under General H. H. Sibley, organized in Minnesota, and the other under the Command of General Alfred Sully, the latter organized and outfitted at Sioux City, Iowa.[6]

Henry Hastings Sibley

Henry Hastings Sibley was born in Detroit, Michigan, on February 20, 1811. Prior to the Expedition, Sibley was a clerk for the American Fur Company from 1830 to 1834. He became a partner of the American Fur Company in 1834 and was involved in trading in the Wisconsin and Dakota territories.[7] In 1848, he was elected as a delegate to the Thirtieth Congress, serving as a Territory of Minnesota delegate from 1849 to 1853. He was a member of the Territorial Legislature of Minnesota in 1857, where he served as president. Minnesota was admitted into the Union in 1858 and Sibley became its first governor. He served until 1860.[8] When appointed to head the expedition he was given the title of colonel of the state militia. He was then raised to brigadier general in the United States regular army.[9]

CHAPTER 2: JUNE 1863

Early in June 1863, General Sibley began assembling his army in what is now Renville County, Minnesota, in the valley of the Minnesota River, three or four miles above the mouth of the Redwood River, at a place he named Camp Pope. When the dust had settled, Sibley commanded an army of 4,075 men. In addition to the Sixth Minnesota under Colonel William Crooks, Sibley had nine companies of the Seventh Minnesota under Lieutenant Colonel William R. Marshall; eight companies of the Tenth Minnesota under Colonel James H. Baker; one company of Pioneers under Captain Jonathan Chase; nine companies of the First Minnesota Cavalry, or Mounted Rangers, under Colonel Samuel McPhail; eight pieces of artillery with one hundred and forty-eight men under Captain John Jones; seventy-five Indian scouts under Major Joseph R. Brown, George McLeoud and Major J. Dooley, in all 4,075 men. The general's staff, whose names would be memorialized on the expedition's camps were R. C. Olin, Assistant Adjutant General; William H. Forbes, Brigade Commissary; Charles B. Atchison, Assistant Commissary and Ordnance Officer; Spencer, Commissary Clerk, Captain Edward Corning, Quartermaster; and Captain William H. Kimball, Assistant Quartermaster. Aides-de-Camp were Lieutenants Pope, F. J. H. Beever, A. St. Claire, S.C. Flandrau, and A. Hawthorn. Rev. S. R. Riggs was chaplain. The guide was Pierre Bottineau.[10]

Around 4:00 a.m. on June 16, 1863, the command began forming for the march with a column of men, weapons, wagons and a large herd of beef cattle, which would supply the army over the winter months.[11] By noon, Camp Pope was almost deserted. The Sibley expedition had begun.

The first day's march was without incident. The weather was

Monument at Fort Ridgely, Camp Pole on the Sibley Expedition.

cool, the troops and animals were fresh, and there were few complaints about heavy knapsacks. After moving only twice the length of the four-mile long train, the expedition halted at a spot near the Minnesota River, eight miles northwest of Fort Ridgely. During the expedition, it was General Sibley's custom to name each camp along the trail for expedition officers. This camp was named for the Sixth Minnesota commander, Colonel William Crooks.[12]

The next day, June 17, the column managed a march of eleven miles before setting up Camp Miller on the site of the Wood Lake Battle. Colonel Marshall, Seventh Minnesota, gave a tour of the battlefield, pointing out where a charge had been made and describing how the battle had been won here the previous September.[13] The following day, the expedition, marching into a fierce wind, passed the ruins of the Upper Agency, crossed the Yellow Medicine River, and camped on Red Iron Creek about 2:00 p.m., a distance of only ten miles from its last camp. The worn-out troops were cheered somewhat by the arrival of the mail. Sibley named the camp Baker.[14] The campsite is in Chippewa County, Minnesota.

On June 19, a cold wet day, the expedition rested and repacked. Dry weather and rough trails had broken up the barrels of hardtack, and the barrels had to be coppered and the hard bread re-

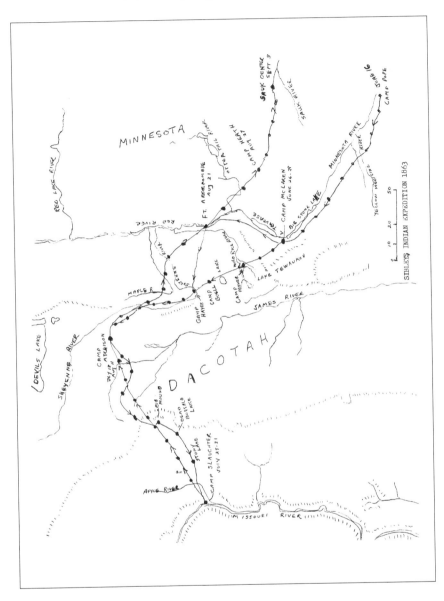

packed.

By all accounts, the June 20 march was terrible. The weather turned cold, there was a steady drizzle, and the entire eighteen miles of the march were against a strong wind. Overcoats were broken out, but the troops still moved around the camp shivering. Sibley named the camp after Colonel Samuel McPhail, First Minnesota Cavalry or Mounted Rangers.[15] The campsite is also in Chippewa County, near

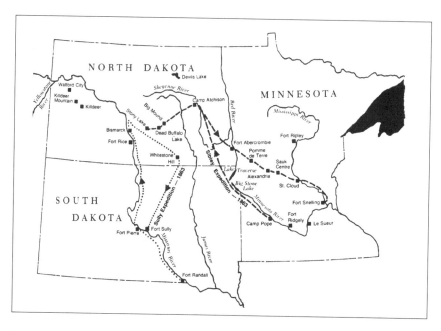

This Map shows the routes of military expeditions in Dakota Territory in 1863-64. Map by Allan Ominsky. Map from: Carley, Kenneth, <u>The Sioux Uprising of 1862</u> (St. Paul, MN: Historical Society, 1976) Page 88.

the Minnesota River.

On Sunday, June 21, Sibley issued an order designating Sunday as a day of rest, an order which was followed throughout the campaign. According to Sibley,

> We shall march farther week after week, by resting on God's day, than we should by marching through the seven. But there is a higher view on the subject. If God be not with us, we shall fail of accomplishing the desired objects, and one way to secure the presence and assistance of God is to remember the Sabbath day to keep it holy.[16]

Just in case God was not watching, however, scouts were sent out to check the countryside for Indians.[17]

On Monday, June 22, the weather and the terrain changed. For the next two days the expedition suffered from the heat and from a lack of water. The prairie was like a desert; the troops' eyes and nostrils suffered greatly and most complained of sunburned faces. The only water available was in slimy green ponds or rapidly drying sloughs, which they had to use or do without. The only bright spot in the two days of marching was the news that after Camp Ramsey, where they stopped on June 22, the soldiers would no longer be required to carry their own knapsacks.[18] The site of Camp Ramsey is in Swift County, Minnesota.

The next day, the troops began the march "with lighter loads and lighter hearts," but the heat and the lack of water began to tell on them:

> The weather is extremely warm, the ground parched, and cracked open in many places, the grass dried up, water to be found only in sloughs, and then offensive and impure; so that before we have made twelve or fifteen miles we are wearied, and we are all glad to come in sight of camp, and then form our line, stack arms, take off our accoutrements, break into columns, and rest! We have been crossing a boundless prairie, which stretches off till it apparently blends with the sky, sometimes, by the action of heat, making a mirage of timber and lakes. The train moves slowly along, rolling up great clouds of dust, and we march along mechanically, glad to drop down and rest whenever the bugle sounds halt! We are camped, again, on a filthy pond, and it is only a mile to a fine stream, the Yellow Earth river.[19]

Camp Averill, which the troops occupied on June 23, was located in Big Stone County.[20]

Up to this point, the scouts had not discovered any Indian

sign, but on Wednesday, June 24, at Camp Marshal on the banks of Abbey and Sarah lakes near Big Stone Lake, an Indian dog was seen, indicating Indians were in the vicinity.[21] No Indians appeared, but a big black ox wandered into camp. He had apparently been left behind by a wagon train the fall before and had wintered-over in the vicinity.[22]

On Thursday, June 25, the expedition skirted Big Stone Lake and set up Camp Jennison on Swan Lake.[23] When a herd of bison was sighted to the west towards a coteau, Private Oscar Garrett Wall and several others, including an officer, left the expedition for an unofficial hunt. Every man in Wall's company had a ration of buffalo steak that evening. The hunters managed to avoid disciplinary action by sharing the kill with their superiors.[24]

The next day, the expedition covered ten miles before establishing Camp McLaren on a level plain between Big Stone Lake and Lake Traverse, the site of Standing Buffalo's village.[25] Big Stone lake stretched thirty-six miles end to end. They were now 116 miles from Camp Pope and had reached the continental divide, where Lake Traverse's waters flow into the Red River of the North and then to Hudson Bay and Big Stone Lake's flow into the Minnesota River and then to the Gulf of Mexico. Indians had occupied the region during the winter and early spring, but had pushed off towards Devils Lake.[26]

Following Sibley's order, the command remained in camp on Sunday, June 28. Guards were posted around the camp to prevent further pillaging of Indian graves. During the expedition, Sibley had problems with soldiers wandering from camp on Sundays. He also used the Sunday rest stops as a opportunity to bring stragglers into camp.

The expedition remained in camp here until June 29. There was a feeling among some of the expedition's members that the extreme drought would prevent any further movement.

After mustering for pay on the morning of June 30, the main column moved northwest eight miles on a well-marked Indian trail that led to the great bend of the Sheyenne river and on to Devils Lake.[27] Camp Bradley, where the main column stopped for the night of June 30, was about eight miles northwest of Browns Valley, Minnesota. The site is approximately one mile off Interstate 29, north of

Camp McLaren
View of Big Stone Lake, present day Browns Valley, Minnesota.
Camp McLaren was located between Big Stone Lake and Lake
Traverse.

View of Lake Traverse, on the border between South Dakota and
Minnesota the detachment traveled along side this lake on the
way to Fort Abercrombie to pick up supplies.

Sisseton, South Dakota.

On the same day, a detachment consisting of Companies H, of the 6th, I of the 7th, H of the 9th, some pioneers and three Companies of the 1st battalion of the Rangers, Companies G, A, and D under the command of Lieutenant Colonel Averill was sent to Fort Abercrombie for supplies.[28] The detachment moved down Lake

Traverse and camped on a wide plain near the lake, which was little more than a swamp filled with filthy water. They made twenty miles, with the troops walking and riding alternately by platoons.[29]

On July 1, the detachment, walking half the time, made about 30 miles before camping on Red River, opposite the ruins of Breckenridge, which had been destroyed and burned by the Sioux on August 23, 1862. Roll call was at 2:30 a.m. and the detachment was moving by 4:30. They kept a steady march, halting only once in a vain attempt to extinguish a fire apparently set by Indians in a thick stand of dead grass. They were "crossing an immense plain, where only land can be seen—one dead level as far in every direction as the eye can reach. We are much fatigued. It is nearly as hard to ride as to walk."[30] Worn out, they made camp.

The detachment reached Fort Abercrombie July 2, where they rested for several days. They found the effects of the drought worse here than elsewhere, but they were still impressed with the condition of the fort:

> The fort is very strong now. The clean airy, quarters look very desirable. I think most of us would be willing to exchange our tramp for an abode even in this place, remote from civilization. We love to look at the green timber on Red river, and also the groves, which are very plain, on the Wild Rice, 5 or 6 miles off. Bathing in the Red River, drinking ice water in the Fort, and eating soft bread, we are enjoying ourselves. Total distance from Camp McLaren, 65 miles. From Ft. Ridgely, 203 miles.[31]

CHAPTER 3: JULY 1863

On July 1, 1863, the main column moved sixteen miles west and set up Camp Cook on an immense, treeless plain that stretched as far as the eye could see. The site is in the vicinity of Claire City, South Dakota.

The next day, the expedition crossed over into what is now Sargent County in North Dakota, setting up Camp Parker on the eastern end of Lake Tewaukon (Skunk Lake). The camp was named for Major John H. Parker, First Minnesota Rangers.[33] The grasshoppers were thick here, raising concern about the prospects for grazing the

Camp Parker
Located on the northeast side of Lake Tewaukon, six miles south and one and a half miles west of present day Geneseo, North Dakota.

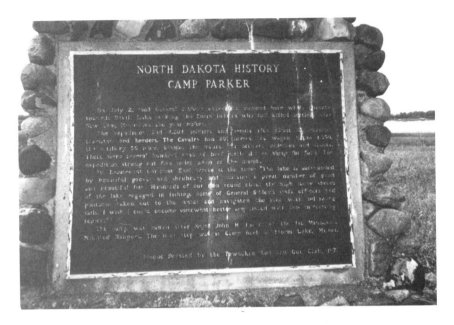

expedition's cattle and fueling further discussion of the possibility that the expedition might fail.[34]

On July 3, the main column crossed the Wild Rice River, continued northwest to the east side of Kandiotta Lake (Buffalo Lake), and then marched almost straight north to the southwest of Storm Lake. The twenty-mile march was very trying on the men: Some of

Camp Buell
Located on the south shore of Storm Lake at present day Milnor,
North Dakota right off Highway 13.

the troops were "completely exhausted and fell down."[35] Camp Buell
was named for Major Salmon E. Buell, First Minnesota Mounted
Rangers. The site is at Milnor, North Dakota. Colonel Marshall, Seventh Minnesota, wrote in his diary that they camped near a miserable
shallow green lake. Because the lake water was unfit for use, the
men dug wells near the lake to get water. Often on the expedition the
soldiers had to strain their water through sand and then disguise the
taste with strong coffee. Several buffalo were sighted that day. Today, Camp Buell and Camp Parker are designated as state historical
sites.

From here the main column went northwest twelve miles and
crossed the Sheyenne River three or four miles below the great bend,
where they set up Camp Hayes on Independence Day, July 4.

Camp Hayes, named for Major Oren T. Hayes, was located
on the "north bank on a plateau opposite two artificial mounds on the
top of the bluff on south side." The soldiers dug into one of the
mounds, finding human bones in sitting positions and decayed pieces
of wood ten feet below the surface. They judged the burial site pre-
dated the contemporary Indian races. They also discovered the site
of an abandoned Sheyenne village on the south side of the river, three

or four miles below the camp.[36] In 1842, the Cheyennes and Pottawattomies fought a battle at this site. During the battle, the Pottawattomies were driven to the table-land and the party there was nearly exterminated in a battle that lasted a whole afternoon. The site is about eight miles south of Lisbon, North Dakota.[37]

For trooper Oscar Wall, "This was indeed a strange Fourth of July. No man in the command had ever before seen one like it. No mark of civilization had ever been raised in this country. No surveys had been made. No white man had disturbed the solitude in which we had entered. Herds of buffalo were visible in almost any direction. Aside from these nothing was seen but arched skies and boundless prairie." [38]

On the evening of the Fourth, salutes were fired, and there were toasts, speeches, and singing. Some of the field and staff officers were invited to General Sibley's tent to sample a fruit cake sent along by Mrs. Sibley for the occasion.[39] A tall Liberty Pole of white ash was erected and the states and territories were saluted with 39 shots from the artillery.[40]

The expedition remained here until July 11, waiting for the detachment to return from Fort Abercrombie. The author's great-grandfather Frank Heath and grandfather Earl Heath once farmed

Camp Hayes
Photo taken on a high hill on the south side of the Sheyenne River, looking north. The field beyond the tree line is where Camp Hayes is located. Camp Hayes is located in the south 1/2 Section 36-134-55, Big Bend Township, eight miles southeast of Lisbon.

the land where Camp Hayes was located. All that was left at that time was a rock site and evidence of entrenchments made in 1863. The present landowner bulldozed the site and now farms on top of it.

The expedition continued to be plagued by northern plains weather. For the detachment returning from Fort Abercrombie, July 7 was "a day long to be remembered."

> The hot beams of the sun poured down on us, without cessation; no air stirring, and we have sweltered in the burning heat. It would have fatigued us to make a common march, and we have made 20 miles. I think we never realized the priceless value of good water more than today, when we found the clear spring brook which empties into the Sheyenne. We are camped [Tattersall] near the river.[41]

Thursday, July 8, was worse.

> The pioneers and a large detail of the different companies, were busy last night till dark, and till 9 this morning, digging down the banks and partially filling up the river, so that the train could cross. Then by attaching ropes, and with the help of a large number pulling, the train was successfully drawn over, and all started. We supposed we had only about 10 miles to

march. At noon we had reached a fine
spring brook, where beavers had
worked busily, which we called Bea-
ver Creek. Fine water. We might have
camped there, but there was no forage
for the teams. We came on and on, and
finally at nearly sun down camped on
a bluff, near the river [Camp Wilson].
Must have made 18 miles. A few more
such marches would use up this detachment.[42]

**Arthur M. Daniels, <u>A Journal of Sibley's Indian Expedition Dur-
ing the Summer of 1863 and Record of the Troops Employed: By
a Soldier in Company "H", 6th Regiment.</u> (Minneapolis, MN:
James D. Thueson, 1980), p. IV-V. (Camp Hayes)**

On July 9, the detachment reached Camp Hayes, where the
main column had been camped since July 4. The detachment had
marched 121 miles and was fifty-six miles from Fort Abercrombie.
It was still so hot the tents were like ovens and there was no other
shelter. According to one account of the expedition, temperatures
hovered around the 100 degree mark, with at least one occasion when
it was 111 degrees in the shade.[44]

The next day, the wind shifted, raising a dust and bringing in
smoke from forests fires in northern Minnesota. Again, questions
were raised about the future of the expedition, with some speculat-

ing that because of the drought it was hardly possible for the march to continue.[45]

Then, on July 11, the heat broke and the men needed their overcoats.

When the march resumed on July 11, the expedition moved in closer columns, with regiments on both sides of the wagon train to secure it against any sudden attack. As a further precaution, the camps were entrenched each night. They traveled fifteen miles and made Camp Wharton on a bluff on the east side of the Sheyenne River. In his journal, Private Henry Hagadorn described the site as the most beautiful scenery he had seen during the expedition.[46] At Camp Wharton, the troops were able to send letters home by Chippewa scouts at a cost of ten cents for soldiers' and twenty-five cents for officers' letters. There may have been questions about the actual cost, because Daniels added the cryptic comment, "At least, these were the charges made by Harry Balcom of the 7th regiment."[47] They remained here for two days. The site of the camp, which was named for Dr. Alfred Wharton, Sixth Minnesota Volunteer Infantry, is about five miles northwest of Lisbon, North Dakota.[48]

On Monday, July 13, they broke camp at 4:00 a.m. to avoid the heat and marched thirteen miles, reaching their next campsite at 9:00 a.m.

This campsite was named for Dr. Joseph H. Weiser, Surgeon, First Minnesota Mounted Rangers, who was killed at the Battle of Big Mound. The site is about four miles southwest of Nome/ Highway 32 Junction, on the Storhoff farm.[49]

To avoid the heat, the march began early on Tuesday, July 14. After an eighteen-mile march, they made camp about one and one-half miles from the Sheyenne River, naming the camp for Dr. Samuel B. Sheardown, Tenth Minnesota Infantry.[50] A bronze tablet marks the site of the camp.

Another march of twelve miles brought the column to a shallow, horseshoe-shaped lake named Tolac or Tolic. The lake looked fine, but the water was "mean tasting."[51] As a result, several wells were dug. The shallow lake is thought to have been near present-day Valley City, North Dakota, but it has long since disappeared as the result of cultivation. They named the camp after Dr. Lucius B. Smith, Sixth Regiment surgeon.[52]

Camp Sheardown
This camp is located three miles south of present day Valley City,
North Dakota, in the northwest 1/4 Section 2-139-58, Marsh
Township and is marked by this bronze tablet.

From Camp Smith, the column moved in a nearly northern
direction. After a march of ten miles, they reached the Sheyenne River,
where discipline, to a certain extent, broke down. Someone spotted
an elk, and before long the prairie was dotted with horsemen chasing
the solitary animal. A Captain Taylor is said to have finally killed the
elk by running it through with his cavalry saber.

When the expedition reached the bluff overlooking the river,
an unexpected scene stretched before them:

> When we reached the bluff, both be-
> fore and behind we had a beautiful
> scene stretched out before us. At our
> feet and winding around among the
> bluffs up and down as far as the eye
> could reach, its course plainly distin-
> guished by the line of timber, so richly
> green and luxuriant was the Sheyenne.
> Our position was commanding, and the

vision extended for miles over the bluff and prairies, a broken country, stretching away till nothing could be discerned—but a dim outline against the hazy sky. At our left, behind, the long train was stretched out in two ranks and in a perfect line, the white canvas coverings, "prairie schooners," stretching off south as far as the eye could reach. The 7th and 10th regiments—solid columns—were coming up on opposite sides of the train, and-right before us, the advance guard, infantry and cavalry, were winding up the steep bluffs on the other side.[53]

Passing up an opportunity to make camp in a cool, shady grove, the officers led the columns across the river about four miles, to a "miserable, nasty, muddy pond." "Only a step," Daniels commented, "from the sublime to the ridiculous."[54] They named the place Camp Corning. Captain Edward Corning was quartermaster on Sibley's staff. The site is on Barnes County 19, at the Sibley Crossing turn, about seven miles northeast of Dazey, North Dakota. A gran-

Camp Corning
This site is located in the southeast 1/4 Section 7-143-58, Sibley Township, about seven miles northeast of Dazey, North Dakota.

ite monument marks the site.[55]

The following day after a fatiguing sixteen-mile hike, they set up Camp Pope on another frog pond. An Indian was brought into camp by two of the rear guard, who had apparently been left behind when they decided to take a nap. How they acquired the Indian is not clear. Captain Douglas Pope, for whom the camp was named, was a member of Sibley's staff and, later became Sibley's son-in-law when he married Augusta Sibley, the general's eldest daughter. Six hundred seventy-six men camped here.[56]

There was a rumor that cavalry had made contact with Indians and was in pursuit of them.

Saturday, July 18, was cloudy, with a strong wind and rain. The expeditions first blood was shed this day, when Lieutenant Albert R. Field of Company G, Mounted Rangers, shot a private soldier. The soldier was not seriously wounded. The goal was Lake Jessie, a small lake named by the explorer Fremont. When they reached the vicinity of Lake Jessie, they turned left and made Camp Atchison on a lake Daniels says they named "Emily."[57] The camp was named for Captain Charles B. Atchison, an aide to Major General John Pope on temporary assignment to Sibley. The Camp Atchison state historic site is located on the northeast shore of Lake Sibley, four miles south of Binford, North Dakota.[58]

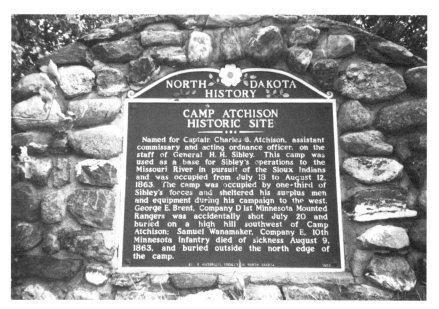

NORTH DAKOTA
HISTORY

CAMP ATCHISON
HISTORIC SITE
• • •

Named for Captain Charles B. Atchison, assistant commissary and acting ordnance officer, on the staff of General H. H. Sibley. This camp was used as a base for Sibley's operations to the Missouri River in pursuit of the Sioux Indians and was occupied from July 13 to August 12, 1863. The camp was occupied by one-third of Sibley's forces and sheltered his surplus men and equipment during his campaign to the west. George E. Brent, Company D 1st Minnesota Mounted Rangers was accidentally shot July 20 and buried on a high hill southwest of Camp Atchison; Samuel Wanamaker, Company E, 10th Minnesota Infantry died of sickness August 9, 1863, and buried outside the north edge of the camp.

STATE HISTORICAL SOCIETY OF NORTH DAKOTA   1962

Camp Atchison Historic Site

In his diary entry for Sunday, July 19, 1863, General Sibley wrote, "Remained in camp. Sunday. Messengers from Fort Abercrombie brought letters for me, and the *Press* of the eighth, announcing *the death of my son Frank*." On June 13, three days before the launching of the expedition, Sibley had received word of the death of his daughter Mamie.[59]

Camp Atchison
**This pasture is where part of the main camp was located, from
July 18 to August 11, 1863. Camp Atchison is located on the north-
east shore of Lake Sibley, nine miles east of Cooperstown, North
Dakota on Highway 200 and then five miles north on Highway 1.
Today this camp is a state historic site.**

At Camp Atchison, they were told that they would not be
going to Devils Lake, but would go instead to the James River and
Coteau du Missouri, where the Indians were reported to be.[60]
The heat, the drought, the extensive prairie fires, and the
plagues of grasshoppers had led many, from the expedition's begin-
ning, to predict that the expedition would fail. General Sibley, how-
ever, was determined to succeed. When he learned that a number of
Indians were heading for the Missouri River, he decided to move
west, rather than north to Devils Lake, where it was believed Little
Crow and around 2,000 Upper Sioux had regrouped after the Wood
Lake Battle. On July 17, Sibley received a dispatch from Camp
Douglas on Devils Lake that Sioux leaders Standing Buffalo,
Mahtowakkon, Red Plume, and Sweet Corn, with six hundred lodges,
had moved west and were making for the Missouri River.
On July 20, Sibley was visited by a group of Métis accompa-
nied by a Catholic Priest named Father André. Certain now that the
information received from Camp Douglas was correct, Sibley held a

war council. The plan was to leave the troops not fit for a forced march those of Companies C and I of the 7th, D of the 10th and C and G of the 6th with cavalry and a section of battery at Camp Atchison, with sufficient guard, and attempt to head off the Indians before they could reach the Missouri.[61] "I am bearing farther west," he wrote in his diary, "to enable me to strike either toward the Coteau of the Missouri, where the Indians are reported to be, or Devil's Lake, as the position of the Indians may render necessary."[62]

The command, now reduced to 1,436 infantry, 520 cavalry, 100 pioneers, artillery, and a number of wagons loaded with 25 days' rations, left immediately.[63] Sibley, injured after a riding accident, made the trip in a buggy or ambulance.[64] On Monday, July 20, the expedition went twenty-three miles without water and established Camp Forbes, named for Captain William H. H. Forbes, Brigade Commissary.[65]

They rested on Sunday. In his diary for this date, Captain John Winthrop Burnham noted, "A cavalry officer shot himself with his carbine while lying in his tent. The ball passed through his body and has likely killed him." [66]

The Forbes campsite is located about six miles south of Juanita, North Dakota.[67] In his diary, George Brackett, one of the Sibley's soldiers, described the camp:

> We marched twenty miles through a
> beautiful country but the lakes were
> dry and we suffered for water. Late in
> the day about 125 men from the Red
> River hunters' camp, an armed band
> of Chippewa half-breeds, rode in with
> a man by the name of Wilkie as their
> leader. They carried the U.S. flag and
> were accompanied by a priest, named
> Andre, who acted as interpreter. He
> had with him a boy ransomed from the
> Indians, who was captured at Old
> Crossing above Breckenridge last year,
> where his parents were murdered.
> These hunters have their families along
> with them, and they dry the buffalo

meat and make pemmican. Their camp
and carts, as well as themselves, are
curiosities. They report the Indians
twenty or more miles distant and that
they will fight for Little Crow and his
band.[68]

Trooper Dana Wright reported the death of George E. Brent
of Company D, 1st Minnesota Mounted Rangers, the first recorded
death in Foster County:

One of the soldiers, George E. Brent,
went to visit the camp of the Chippewa
Indians, enemies of the Sioux, who had
a camp three miles west—on the west
side of the James River. When the Indians returned to their camp that
evening, several of the soldiers went
back with them. Evidently there was
liquor for one soldier in dismounting
from his horse on his return to the soldier camp, caught his riding spur in his
carbine and discharged it, the ball passing through his body. He started back
to Camp Atchison, near Lake Jessie,
the permanent camp for Sibley's men,
but he died before they had gone but a
short distance, dying within the territory that is now Foster County. He was
buried near Jessie, North Dakota.[69]

After breaking camp on July 21, the expedition stopped at
the hunters' camp so the soldiers could trade for moccasins, dried
meat, and buckskin garments before resuming the march. Burnham
described the camp:

It is arranged in style in a circle, their
carts all around the outside. They use
tepees like our Sibley tents. These men
all speak French and are a mixture of
Indian, French and Scotch, each pre-
dominating in the order named. They

are quick and active. Are splendid
horsemen and have good, large and
well-trained horses. We stopped an
hour by their camp to trade but were
not allowed to go in. The trade was
buffalo robes, moccasins, gloves on
their part and tobacco, sugar and blan-
kets on ours. We did not have half time
enough as they were rather shy of Government notes, the only pay we could
well spare.[70]

That night they camped on a rough spot of ground at the head
of one of the lakes through which the James River flows.[71] Camp
Olin was named for Captain Rolin C. Olin, who had been a 2nd Lieutenant in the 3rd Minnesota Infantry. Captured by the Confederates
on July 19, 1862, he had been formally exchanged and returned to
Minnesota. He was promoted to Captain May 11, 1863, and assigned
to General Sibley's staff. The Olin campsite is about midway between Kensal and Bordulac, North Dakota.[72]

On Wednesday July 22 a captured Indian reported that the
Sioux had escaped across the Missouri River. A council of war then
decided the expedition would push on to the Missouri.

On July 22, the expedition advanced twenty miles and made
Camp Kimball on a level plain near a range of timbered bluffs.[73] The
camp could have been named for Surgeon General James P. Kimball
of Fort Buford or for Captain William H. Kimball, General Sibley's
Assistant Quartermaster. Captain William H. Kimball was in charge
of the pontoon train, which was equipped to lay temporary bridges
over streams. They had little to do that dry summer. Little is known
of Kimball's personal history.[74]

In anticipation of an Indian attack, the camp was trenched
and pickets were posted at night. In his diary, Brackett complained
about the lack of news on the progress of the Civil War:

We crossed the James River and its
branch now known as the Pipestem.
Very little water in either stream. Mail
today with St. Paul papers to July 11,
but there was no word of the great vic-

tories won at Gettysburg and Vicksburg some days before.[75]

During the Kimball encampment, Sibley's Indian scouts became nervous, sensing the expedition was nearing the Sioux, although none of the scouts had encountered any. Later it was learned that the Sioux were camped just south of Pettibone.

Today this site is a state historic site and is five miles southwest of Carrington.[76]

In 1902, a homesteader named John Imler plowed up a saber in a field just north of the Kimball campsite. During a visit to North Dakota in 1925, a veteran of the Sibley campaign, John G. Grems of Maryville, Missouri, speculated the sword might have belonged to soldier-of-fortune Lieutenant Frederick John Holt Beever. Beever, an English Oxford-educated nobleman and ordained Anglican clergyman, had signed on with Sibley and had been given the rank of Lieutenant in the Seventh Minnesota Infantry. On July 29, 1863, Beever was ambushed near Apple Creek as he returned from delivering dispatches from Sibley to Colonel William Crooks.

On July 23, reveille was at 3:00 a.m., and the march began at five. Captain Burnham described the march:

> Reveille at 3, started at 5 a.m.
> Marched 18 miles, the first four miles over a pretty level prairie country. We crossed the last of the branches of the James River and began to ascend the "Coteau." We passed a high hill partially covered with timber, and known as "Chief Hill." It stands on the edge of the Coteau. The land became more rough and stony and the last ten miles was the roughest land I have seen for years. We camped on a lake several miles long, known as Long Lake. It winds around among the hills and is very picturesque.
>
> These hills are steep and rocky and the valleys between are full of small lakes now nearly all dry. The

ridges are very dry and entirely desti-
tute of grass, and the valleys are full
of a heavy grass, the best growth we
have seen.

I was very tired tonight. Our fare
has become very poor, the weather is
hot and the march is hard.

The boys caught plenty of ducks
and geese in the reeds around and in
the lakes. The old ones are shedding
their feathers and cannot fly, neither
can the young ones. They could go
faster or the water than a man could
not in the thick grass and reeds.[77]

The site of the encampment, which was named for Captain
Hiram P. Grant, is five miles northwest of Woodworth, North Dakota.[78] Since they were now in Sioux country, the camp was entrenched and well-picketed.[79]

At about noon on Friday, July 24, after traveling twenty miles,
the expedition came upon a large body of Indians. Steps were then
taken to entrench the camp, which they named for their commander.
The Battle of Big Mound took place near the camp where 5,000 Indians had made their home.[80] The camp's exact location is not known,
but the battle is commemorated in the Burman Historic Site, on land
donated by John Burman, who homesteader here in 1906.[81]

As the Indians began to gather, the Mounted Rangers' Surgeon, Dr. J. S. Weiser, rode out of camp to shake hands with the
Indians, many of whom he had known from his home town of
Shakopee, Minnesota, where they had once been frequent visitors.
One of the Indians, possibly a young member of Inkpaduta's band,
shot Dr. Weiser in the back, killing him instantly. An Indian scout
named Stevens was also injured during this incident.[82]

Camp Sibley
This photo was taken on top of McPhails Butte, looking west to
where Camp Sibley was located. Camp Sibley is now under water due to the rising level of a near by lake.

McPhails Butte
Located in the same area as Big Mound and Camp Sibley. It was
near this spot that Dr. Weiser was killed and where the Battle of
Big Mound took place.

McPhails Butte

Monument for Dr. J. S. Weiser
Dr. J.S. Weiser was killed here on July 24, 1863. This event started the Battle of Big Mound. The events of this day are commemorated at the Burman Historic Site in the northwest 1/4 Section 24-141-77, Buckeye Township.

Big Mound
Big Mound is located ten miles north of present day Tappen, North Dakota.

CHAPTER 4: BIG MOUND AND OTHER BATTLES

The shooting of Dr. Weiser precipitated the battle of Big Mound. At 1:00 p.m., with the Sioux encircling the camp, General Sibley gave the order to corral the train on a nearby salt lake and throw up earthworks to protect the wagons. Precisely at 3 p.m., to the accompaniment of a violent prairie thunderstorm, Colonel McPhail's First Cavalry Battalion, supported by two companies of the Seventh regiment, was ordered to advance to hold the ground where Weiser had fallen and divide the opposing force. Colonel Crooks' Sixth regiment, with part of the Seventh, was deployed to protect the right flank and Lieutenant Colonel Averill's two companies shielded the left. With the cavalry now dismounted because of the rough terrain, Colonel Marshall, with five companies of the Seventh, was deployed in the ravine on the left of the cavalry. Part of the Tenth regiment, Colonel Baker commanding, was held in reserve in camp.

Meanwhile, General Sibley, supported by one company of Captain Edgerton's Tenth regiment, opened fire with a six-pounder loaded with spherical case shot from a vantage point overlooking the Sioux in the upper part of the ravine, then ordered a general advance. The Sioux, which Sibley estimated to be about 1,500, were forced southward, closely pursued by Colonel McPhail, supported by the Seventh regiment, part of the Tenth, and Whipple's section battery.

The noise of battle was accompanied by the fierce summer thunderstorm. One private was killed by lightning and a close strike knocked Colonel McPhail's saber out of his hand.[83] Besides the trooper killed by lightning, the expedition listed two killed and two wounded.[84] One of the casualties was Minnesota Mounted Rangers Lieutenant Ambrose Freeman, who had been hunting with George

Brackett, a Minneapolis beef contractor, when the battle began. Brackett, who escaped, turned up seven days later at Camp Atchison, ninety or one hundred miles away.

According to Brackett's account of the incident, Freeman, an avid hunter, frequently left his detachment to hunt with Brackett. Late in the afternoon of July 24, Brackett and Freeman had succeeded in roping a young bison, and after the long chase made plans for another hunt the next day.

The July 25 hunt went well, but in pursuing an antelope, which they killed, the hunters rode well away from the camp. As they returned, with Freeman carrying his half of the dressed carcass draped around his shoulders, they met a small band of Indians, which they initially mistook for cavalry. Freeman was killed as he tried to unload the carcass and get to his musket. Brackett escaped and eventually made it to Camp Atchison.

In 1896, a hunting knife with the name, A. Freeman, carved on it was found in a plowed field near Devils Lake. Supposedly, it had been dropped by one of the men involved in Freeman's death.

The Sioux loss was listed as eighty killed and wounded. Twenty-one of the Sioux casualties had been scalped. The trail was strewn with all manner of articles, provisions, clothes, skins, utensils, and furniture. In the pursuit, the infantry reached a point ten miles beyond camp, the cavalry fifteen.

Immediately following the battle, some serious finger-pointing began. In his diary, Burnham described the situation:

> Here was made a mistake fatal to the purposes of the expedition. Had we pushed on and reached the Missouri before the Indians we could have punished them severely but the delay enabled them to get their families over the river, and after the 24th we saw no more Indians except those armed and in fighting trim.
>
> Hot words passed between the partisans of Colonel McPhail and the general. The colonel said he came back

against his will because he was ordered
back. Sibley's friends said the colonel
was ordered to await the coming of the
main army and the orders in camp cor-
responded thereto. Many remarks de-
rogatory to the courage and qualifica-
tion of certain men to command were
passed about. When the result of the
error became fully known the contro-
versy became bitter, but soon after
Lieutenant Beever, an English gentle-
man, the volunteer aid of General
Sibley, who delivered the order, was
killed by the Indians, and the reports
now say, "the mistake was caused by
the incorrect delivery of an order."
Lieutenant Beever being dead cannot
"kick" if misrepresented.[85]

Confusion reigned during the night of July 24, with no one
completely sure what was happening. The Seventh, Company B of
the Tenth, and the cavalry were lost all night, not making it back to
camp until dawn, but by 7:00 a.m. most of the troops had returned.
At noon on Saturday, July 25, the troops broke camp and moved
about four miles into the hills, where they set up Camp Whitney,
which may have been located eight or so miles from Tappen, North
Dakota. The McPhail Butte Historic Site, a three-acre plot, donated
by John DeKrey, Jr., in 1951, commemorates the encampment.[86]

The water at Camp Sibley had been too salty to drink, so
wells were dug to provide water for men and animals. The weather
turned cold and windy.

On Sunday after marching for an hour and a half they came
to an Indian camp. When the report came that the Sioux were close,
preparations were made to receive an attack from any direction. Continuing the march for another ten miles, they reached Dead Buffalo
Lake, where they found the Sioux ready for battle. At first, the fight-
ing was long range because the Indians refused to close with the
soldiers. An attempt by the Sioux to flank the left side of the camp
and run off the mules failed as the Mounted Rangers and infantry

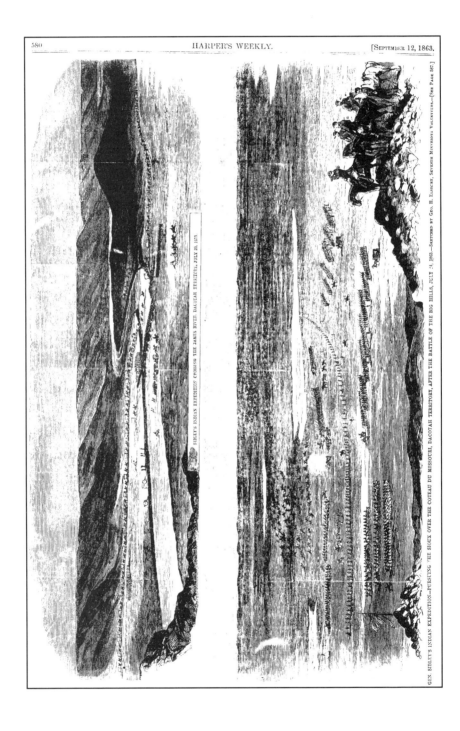

SIBLEY'S INDIAN EXPEDITION CROSSING THE JAMES RIVER, DACOTAH TERRITORY, JULY 26, 1863.

GEN. SIBLEY'S INDIAN EXPEDITION—PURSUING THE SIOUX OVER THE COTEAU DU MISSOURI, DACOTAH TERRITORY, AFTER THE BATTLE OF THE BIG HILLS, JULY 24, 1863.—SKETCHED BY GEO. H. ELSBURY, SEVENTH MINNESOTA VOLUNTEERS.—[SEE PAGE 587.]

fought off the attack. Following this setback, the Sioux retreated, and the expedition went into camp, which they named Pfaender. The camp's namesake and location are unknown.

On Monday, following the battle of Dead Buffalo Lake, Sibley resumed the march, making about twenty miles before his exhausted animals forced him to encamp.[87] Camp Schoenemann was named for Captain Rudolph Schoenemann. It was probably located west of Driscoll, North Dakota.[88] Sibley was told he was now within fifteen miles of the Missouri. As they broke camp, the soldiers spotted a large number of Sioux moving toward them. The Sioux had evidently planned a surprise attack on the camp. Sibley ordered the men to make defensive preparations and to continue the march. As the columns advanced, the Sioux probed for weak spots in the soldiers' positions. Finding none, they rode off and kept out of sight the rest of the day. In his report, Sibley remarked that the Battle of Stony Lake, the official designation for the day's action, was "the greatest conflict between our troops and the Indians, so far as the numbers were concerned."[89] Sibley's officers estimated that from 2,000 to 2,500

Driscoll Sibley Park
The park is located two miles west of present day Driscoll, North Dakota on a paved road. Camp Schoenemann and the Battle of Stony Lake were located near this park.

Indians were involved, a force made up not only of Lower Sissetons, but a number of Yantons and Tetons as well.

The Stony Lake Battle was fought about one mile northeast of the campsite.

On July 28, the expedition traveled eighteen miles and camped on the Apple River, probably about two miles northwest of Menoken.[89] The camp was named for Captain Charles J. Stees. The soldiers spent most of the night fortifying the camp, then were roused by a 2:00 a.m. reveille.[90] Crossing the Apple took forever, and it was eight o'clock before the timber along the Missouri came into view. By then, it was too late. The calvary and part of the Artillery was sent ahead of the train, they halted at the edge of the woods a mile and a half from the river where they saw the Indians. They had already crossed the river and were waiting on the bluffs in immense numbers. The Indians on the bluffs "were constantly signaling to those at the river by flashing the sun's reflection from a mirror."[91]

When the expedition went into camp at the mouth of Apple Creek, at a place they named Camp Slaughter, at least one of the soldiers had had enough. Reflecting on the marches and counter-marches of the day, Daniels wrote:

Camp Slaughter
The camp was located just above the mouth of Apple Creek, in Section 28-138-80, Lincoln Township, four miles south of present day Bismark. Today the site is named Sibley Park.

Slowly—very slowly we returned to camp. We had now nothing to stimulate us to action, but, on the contrary, the prospect, which was as evident to all as the light of day, was sickening. We had eaten but little, and drank almost nothing since half past three in the morning, and by the time we reached camp late in the afternoon, having marched some four miles from the river, to a broad plateau near Apple River, a seemingly natural place for a strong camp, being twenty feet above the bottom, with a steep descent towards the woods, the men were thoroughly exhausted, and laid down feeling as we had not before. We thought we had not much strength left, but we were soon tested, for very soon the "long-roll," with its quick beating, aroused the camp, and the report "the Indians are coming," went quickly from lip to lip through camp. In less than three minutes the 6th were double-quicking it down the steep descent towards the woods, led by Colonel Crooks, on foot; but the alarm was false, and we went back and laid down again. Thus we have finished another day's toil, and the shades of night, will, we hope, close the scene, for if ever we did, we need sleep. All, I think, are sick of Indians and Indian war. Distance, fifteen miles. - Camp Slaughter.[92]

Lieutenant Beever's body was found the following day, and on July 31, he was given the first Masonic funeral conducted in North Dakota.[93] He had been sent into the woods to deliver an order to Col.

Crooks, which he delivered, but he was ambushed and killed on his return. Private Nicholas Miller of Company K of the Sixth was also killed, when he was separated from his company.[94]

The Camp Slaughter site is just above the mouth of Apple Creek, at Burnt Boat Island, a name referring to an incident during Prince Maximilian's tour of the territory. It is now called Sibley Island.[95]

This campsite marked the end of the Sibley Expedition of 1863. There were hardly enough rations left to make it to Camp Atchison, and the animals were in a state of collapse. Disappointed that General Alfred Sully had not appeared, Sibley decided further pursuit of the Indians was not practical. Before leaving Camp Pope it had been arranged for Sully to meet Sibley on the Missouri, if possible. General Sully, with an army similar in size to Sibley's, was to proceed from Sioux City, Iowa, part of the way by river transports. Sully, however, had been detained by low water on the Missouri River. Rockets were fired on the thirtieth and thirty-first to signal Sully if he happened to be close, but there was no response. The expedition now turned eastward, to return to Minnesota.[97]

On July 31 it was excessively hot, with the temperature in General Sibley's large hospital tent, which was open at both ends, reaching 111 degrees. That night, there was also an attack on the north side of camp occupied by the Tenth Regiment. A mule and two horses were killed and the cattle were stampeded. The stampede was halted by companies of the Tenth and Seventh Regiments. The expedition had expected an attack from the Indians, who had been heard in the woods giving signals at about 10:00 p.m.[98]

CHAPTER 5: AUGUST-SEPTEMBER 1863

On Saturday, August 1, 1863, the return trip began. Following their old trail, the expedition traveled seventeen miles, skirting the site of Camp Sees, before making Camp Braden.[98] It had now been forty-seven days since the men had seen any mark of white settlement.[99] On the Sunday, August 2, they passed Camp Schoenemann, marching twenty miles and making Camp Banks.[100] At Camp Banks, Chaska, one of the Sioux scouts, became violently ill and died.[101]

There were a number of Native Americans named Chaska in the Minnesota area, and finding which Chaska is which is nearly impossible. However, it is known that Little Crow had a lieutenant called Chaska. His real name was Wakinyatawa, "His Thunder," and he was spared from hanging with other Sioux because he had saved the life of George Spencer, a Minnesota trader. When Sibley was organizing his expedition, Chaska signed on as a scout.

When the command went into camp, according to one account, Chaska went to the surgeon for liniment to relieve a back pain. The surgeon's assistant and Chaska shared a quick drink and Chaska returned to his tent. About 10:00 p.m. an officer was informed that Chaska and the assistant were having seizures. The surgeon's assistant survived, Chaska didn't.

When the incident was investigated, it was discovered that the alcohol they shared had been consumed from an improperly-washed bottle that once contained strychnine. Conspiracy theory buffs suspect foul play, but Chaska's death was probably nothing more than the result of medical carelessness.

Chaska was buried August 3, 1863, at Camp Banks. The Camp Chaska Historical Site marks the spot.

August 3 was, as Daniels put it, "One of those days which we have only on the western plains—a perfect tornado of wind all day

Camp Banks
On the return trip, Chaska a Sioux scout, died at this site on August 2, 1863. The Camp Chaska Historical Site is located in the southwest 1/4 Section 34-140-75, Clear Lake Township, three miles north of present day Driscoll, North Dakota, just north of the probable site of Camp Banks.

from the south."[102] They traveled only sixteen miles before setting up Camp Kennedy near a spring General Sibley named Crystal Springs.[103] The camp was named for Captain John Kennedy. The site is not marked.

They reached Big Mound on the fourth. They marched seventeen miles, passing Camp Sibley on the way and named the next camp for Captain William C. Williston. The unmarked site was probably on Kunkle Lake.[104]

On Wednesday, August 5, they rested. About 9:00 a.m. the following day, camp was thrown into confusion when scouts reported that the surrounding bluffs were full of Indians. The "hoards" turned out to be Métis from Camp Atchison, bringing mail.[105] They also brought the report that beef contractor Brackett was safe at Atchison.

On Thursday, August 6, the expedition moved eighteen miles in a northeasterly direction, passing Camp Grant and making camp among some "miserable alkaline" lakes.[106] Captain James Gilfillan's name was chosen for this camp, which was located six miles from Woodworth, North Dakota.[107]

On Friday, August 7, they advanced eighteen miles, passing Camp Kimball and setting up Camp Hall. A lone bison was spotted.

He kept his distance ahead of the train for a long time before finally running off. The camp was close to a half-breed camp and some of the Métis visited the troops. About a dozen Indians were captured and some were sent to Fort Snelling.[108] Named for Captain Thomas G. Hall, the site is about midway between Melville and Bordulac, North Dakota.[109]

Still moving in a northeasterly direction, they covered about twelve miles, passing Camp Olin on their right before crossing the James River. Camp Carter, named for Captain Theo. G. Carter, was about two miles from Camp Forbes and 25 miles from Camp Atchison. After a regimental inspection at 9:00 a.m. on Sunday, August 9, they marched a short distance from the camp and fired their muskets, which had remained loaded since the battles of Big Mound, Dead Buffalo Lake, and Stony Lake.

On Monday, August 10, they reached Camp Atchison, the main camp, 125 miles from the Missouri River. Averaging about eighteen miles a day, they had covered the 125 miles in seven days. When they reached camp, they were given a soldiers' welcome and served a royal supper of baked beans, fried hardtack, and coffee.[110] The returning soldiers noted that, to pass the time, the Camp Atchison troops had amused themselves by making rings and other trinkets from bison horns.

On the morning of August 12, 1863, Camp Atchison passed out of existence. General Sibley returned with the main body of the expedition by the former trail as far as the big bend in the Sheyenne River, then to Fort Abercrombie, and finally to Fort Snelling. Colonel McPhail, with companies B, E, F, I, and M of the cavalry, went southward west of the Sheyenne. There was a rumor that Colonel McPhail's Mounted Rangers were going to Snake River country with a wheelbarrow load of provisions. McPhail's men were furious. They had no idea where Snake River country was.[111]

Colonel McPhail and the Mounted Rangers went down along the James River to scout for Indians of Sleepy Eye's band.[112] They went by the site of present-day Fort Ransom and may have passed close by Stirum on the way to their old trail.[113] On August 22, they found the trail and, to their relief, realized the Snake River rumor had been wrong. On the twenty-fourth, they camped at Big Stone Lake in Minnesota. They arrived at Fort Ridgely on September 1.[114]

The Mounted Rangers had made the trip in a short time, much shorter than they had anticipated.

Meanwhile, the main expedition went eighteen miles on August 12 and made Camp Burt (for Captain William C. Burt) on a green lake, where they dug wells for water. The site is about two miles northeast of Hannaford, North Dakota.[115] That night they dug what would be the last entrenchments of the expedition. On the thirteenth, they went seventeen miles, passed Camp Corning, and made it to Camp Libby three miles south of the Sheyenne. It had only been a month or so since they last crossed the Sheyenne.[116]

At Camp Libby, which was named for Captain Asa Libby, Jr., a private named Kristian Peterson died of fever. Kristian and his four brothers—John, Hans, Peter, and Nels—were Norwegian immigrants who had settled near Willmar, Minnesota, in 1859, and all five enlisted as privates in Troop D, Minnesota First Cavalry after President Lincoln's call for volunteers. After Kristian's death the brothers fabricated a rude casket from an old wagon box, dug a deep grave, and marked the site with rocks. In 1929, the grave was discovered and a military memorial service was conducted by the Cooperstown and

Camp Arnold
Two soldiers of Sibley's Expedition died and were buried here on August 15, 1863. This site is located four miles north of Oriska, North Dakota on Highway 32.

Camp Arnold

Hannaford, North Dakota, American Legion posts.[117]

On Friday, August 14, they marched thirteen miles in a cold wind and named their camp for Captain John K. Arnold. The next day, which was much warmer, they went twelve miles and made Camp (Albert H.) Stevens on a muddy lake, where wells were again dug. On Sunday they rested. On August 17, another warm day, they crossed the dry bed of a branch of the Maple River. They made sixteen miles that day. The site for Camp Ambler, which was named for Captain Rufus C. Ambler, is located on the Maple River, a plot of ground donated by landowner Alvin Zaeske is now a historic site.[118] They rested on Sunday, August 18, and resumed the homeward march on the nineteenth, moved seventeen miles, and named their next camp for Captain Jonah Chase.[119]

On August 20 they accomplished only four miles, making Camp Edgerton, named for Captain Alonzo J. Edgerton, on a little rush pond. On Friday, August 21, after a sixteen-mile march, they reached Fort Abercrombie by way of the Wild Rice River. Camp Hackett, named for Captain Charles W. Hackett, was located in or near Fort Abercrombie. This was the expedition's last camp in what is now North Dakota. They were now 113 miles from Camp Atchison and 238 miles from the Missouri River. Company H of the Ninth and Company L of the Rangers stayed at Fort Abercrombie. Companies A, D, and G went on to Fort Ripley.[120]

On Tuesday, August 25, the men again set out for home. They went eleven miles up the Red River and made Camp Phelps, near the location of Breckenridge, Minnesota. The next day, August 26, they marched twenty-six miles, twenty without water, and made Camp White. On the way, they passed a shanty and the remains of destroyed buildings. Thursday, August 27, they went fifteen miles and made Camp Heath among some lakes and near wood. They were near Pomme de Terre.[121]

On the August 28, they went eighteen miles, crossed the Pomme de Terre River and made Camp Sullivan. On Saturday, August 29, they traveled fifteen miles, and when they made Camp O'Connor, the restrictions against hunting were partially removed. They rested on the thirtieth. On the August 31, they went eighteen miles and made Camp Jones.[122]

On Tuesday, September 1, they went seventeen miles and made Camp Beever on Jones Lake on a plat laid out for the town of Westport, Minnesota, twelve miles from Sauk Centre. On the second, they began to pass the farms and houses of white settlers. They made Camp Rubles at Sauk Centre, they had their first break from the soldiers' diet of hardtack and bad water, a "white meal of biscuits, butter, cheese, and milk." They rested on the 3rd. Friday the 4th they traveled eighteen and a half miles and made Camp Wilson. On the 5th they went sixteen miles and made Camp Austin. On Sunday the 6th they rested. Monday September 7th was a severe march of nineteen and a half miles. They were within two and a half miles of Saint Cloud. There they made Camp Taylor. On Tuesday the 8th they went nine miles and made Camp Daniels. General Sibley and Col. Crooks went ahead, leaving Col. Averill in command. On Wednesday the 9th they marched twenty-one miles and made Camp Anderson on Big Lake. Thursday the 10th they traveled nineteen miles and made Camp Davys on high ground near Anoka. On Friday the 11th they were within four miles of St. Anthony (present-day Minneapolis). They went sixteen miles and made Camp Rice.[123]

On Saturday, September 12, 1963, they reached Fort Snelling, having marched 171 miles during September, averaging over 15 miles each day. Their last camp, Camp Steele, was 225 miles from Fort Abercrombie and 493 miles from the Missouri. Since leaving Camp Pope the expedition had traveled 939 miles.

In the last entry in his diary, Lieutenant Daniels expressed the soldiers' relief at being at the end of the adventure:

Saturday, 2 p.m. – At Fort Snelling. Amid familiar sights and the warm embraces of loving friends, at the place where nearly all commenced soldiering, we make our last halt of the expedition, take off our accoutrements, break into column and REST! We for-

Fort Snelling, located at present day St. Paul, Minnesota, Camp Steele on the Sibley Expedition.

Fort Snelling

get our toil in the glad thought that we shall *all* soon be at home.[124]

In the eyes of Sibley's apologists, the expedition was a great success, but as early as 1864 others were decrying both Sibley's and Sully's campaigns as "expensive and useless."[125] Neither campaign, it is true, produced any clear-cut victories. Both armies advanced ponderously, their arrivals heralded by the huge clouds of dust raised by the supply wagons and cattle herds. The Sioux had little trouble evading them. Nevertheless, for the men who accompanied Sibley, it was an exciting time, as John Winthrop Burnham observed upon reflection years later:

> Men who served on this expedition always speak of it as a great affair. It was a long march and we bore trials of fatigue from water and short rations, in a service 500 miles from support and against a foe where it was victory or death. Should we be conquered none of us probably would ever be seen again. The fate that overtook Custer and his Command in later years would have been ours had we been beaten.[126]

The Sibley House, in Mendota, Minnesota. This was the first stone house in Minnesota. Sibley began his fur trading career here in 1834, prior to the Sibley Expedition.

The Sibley House

NOTES

[1] Kenneth Carley, The Sioux Uprising of 1862 (St. Paul, 1976), p. 1-2.

[2] Kenneth Carley, The Sioux Uprising of 1862 (St. Paul, 1976), p. 2.

[3] Kenneth Carley, The Sioux Uprising of 1862 (St. Paul, 1976), p. 2-3.

[4] Kenneth Carley, The Sioux Uprising of 1862 (St. Paul, 1976), p. 3-4.

[5] Kenneth Carley, The Sioux Uprising of 1862 (St. Paul, 1976), p. 5.

[6] Kenneth Carley, The Sioux Uprising of 1862 (St. Paul, 1976), p. 5.

[7] Kenneth Carley, The Sioux Uprising of 1862 (St. Paul, 1976), p. 5-6.

[8] Kenneth Carley, The Sioux Uprising of 1862 (St. Paul, 1976), p. 14.

[9] Oscar Garrett Wall, Recollections of the Sioux Massacre (Lake City, MN, 1908), p. 237-240.

[10] "Sibley, Henry Hastings." n.d. < http://www.bartleby.com/65/e-/E-Sibley-H.html > (29 Jan. 2001).

[11] "Sibley, Henry Hastings, 1811-1891." n.d.. <http://www.bioguide.congress.gov/scripts/biodisplay.pl?index=S000396.html >(29 Jan. 2001).

[12] Soule, H.A. "Early History of Sargent County." Cogswell Enterprise Jan. 29, 1925, p.1.

[13] Oscar Garrett Wall, Recollections of the Sioux Massacre (Lake City, MN, 1908), p. 242-43.

[14] Oscar Garrett Wall, Recollections of the Sioux Massacre (Lake City, MN, 1908), p. 245.

[15] Arthur Daniels, A Journal of Sibley's Indian Expedition During the Summer of 1863 and Record of the Troops Employed/ By a Soldier in Company "H", 6th Regiment (Minneapolis, MN: James D. Thueson, 1980), p. 18.

[16] Oscar Garrett Wall, Recollections of the Sioux Massacre (Lake City, MN, 1908), p. 247.

[17] Arthur Daniels, A Journal of Sibley's Indian Expedition During the Summer of 1863 and Record of the Troops Employed (Minneapolis, 1980), p. 18.

[18] Arthur Daniels, A Journal of Sibley's Indian Expedition During the Summer of 1863 and Record of the Troops Employed (Minneapolis, 1980), p. 18-19.

[19] Oscar Garrett Wall, Recollections of the Sioux Massacre (Lake City, MN, 1908), p. 248.

[20] Arthur Daniels, A Journal of Sibley's Indian Expedition During the Summer of 1863 and Record of the Troops Employed (Minneapolis, 1980), p. 19-20.

[21] Colonel William R. Marshall, Journal of the Military Expedition Against the Sioux Indians from Camp Pope in the Summer of 1863 Under Command of Brigadier General Henry Hastings Sibley (Original journal at the Minnesota Historical Society).

[22] Arthur Daniels, A Journal of Sibley's Indian Expedition During the Summer of 1863 and Record of the Troops Employed (Minneapolis, 1980), p. 20.

[23] Colonel William R. Marshall, Journal of the Military Expedition

Against the Sioux Indians from Camp Pope in the Summer of 1863 Under Command of Brigadier General Henry Hastings Sibley (Original journal at the Minnesota Historical Society).

[24] Arthur Daniels, A Journal of Sibley's Indian Expedition During the Summer of 1863 and Record of the Troops Employed (Minneapolis, 1980), p. 20.

[25] Oscar Garrett Wall, Recollections of the Sioux Massacre (Lake City, MN, 1908), p. 249-50.

[26] Arthur Daniels, A Journal of Sibley's Indian Expedition During the Summer of 1863 and Record of the Troops Employed (Minneapolis, 1980), p. 21.

[27] Oscar Garrett Wall, Recollections of the Sioux Massacre (Lake City, MN, 1908), p. 251.

[28] Oscar Garrett Wall, Recollections of the Sioux Massacre (Lake City, MN, 1908), p. 252.

[29] Colonel William R. Marshall, Journal of the Military Expedition Against the Sioux Indians from Camp Pope in the Summer of 1863 Under Command of Brigadier General Henry Hastings Sibley (Original journal at the Minnesota Historical Society).

[30] Arthur Daniels, A Journal of Sibley's Indian Expedition During the Summer of 1863 and Record of the Troops Employed (Minneapolis, 1980), p. 21.

[31] Oscar Garrett Wall, Recollections of the Sioux Massacre (Lake City, MN, 1908), p. 252.

[32] Arthur Daniels, A Journal of Sibley's Indian Expedition During the Summer of 1863 and Record of the Troops Employed (Minneapolis, 1980), p. 22.

[33] Oscar Garrett Wall, Recollections of the Sioux Massacre (Lake City, MN, 1908), p. 245-46.

[34] Colonel William R. Marshall, Journal of the Military Expedition Against the Sioux Indians from Camp Pope in the Summer of 1863 Under Command of Brigadier General Henry Hastings Sibley (Original journal at the Minnesota Historical Society).

[35] Oscar Garrett Wall, Recollections of the Sioux Massacre (Lake City, MN, 1908), p. 245-46.

[36] Arthur Daniels, A Journal of Sibley's Indian Expedition During the Summer of 1863 and Record of the Troops Employed (Minneapolis, 1980), p. 22-23.

[37] Milnor's 75th Anniversary Community Book 1883-1958 (Milnor, ND, 1958), p. 73.

[38] Colonel William R. Marshall, Journal of the Military Expedition Against the Sioux Indians from Camp Pope in the Summer of 1863 Under Command of Brigadier General Henry Hastings Sibley (Original journal at the Minnesota Historical Society).

[39] Arthur Daniels, A Journal of Sibley's Indian Expedition During the Summer of 1863 and Record of the Troops Employed (Minneapolis, 1980), p. 23.

[40] Colonel William R. Marshall, Journal of the Military Expedition Against the Sioux Indians from Camp Pope in the Summer of 1863 Under Command of Brigadier General Henry Hastings Sibley (Original journal at the Minnesota Historical Society).

[41] Milnor's 75th Anniversary Community Book 1883-1958 (Milnor, ND, 1958), p. 73.

[42] Arthur Daniels, A Journal of Sibley's Indian Expedition During the Summer of 1863 and Record of the Troops Employed (Minneapolis, 1980), p. 23.

[44] Oscar Garrett Wall, Recollections of the Sioux Massacre (Lake City, MN, 1908), p. 255-56.

[45] Colonel William R. Marshall, Journal of the Military Expedition Against the Sioux Indians from Camp Pope in the Summer of 1863 Under Command of Brigadier General Henry Hastings Sibley (Original journal at the Minnesota Historical Society).

[46] Enderlin North Dakota 1891-1966 Diamond Jubilee (Enderlin, ND, 1966) p. 5.

[47] Oscar Garrett Wall, Recollections of the Sioux Massacre (Lake City, MN, 1908), p. 255-56.

[48] Oscar Garrett Wall, Recollections of the Sioux Massacre (Lake City, MN, 1908), p. 255-56.

[49] Arthur Daniels, A Journal of Sibley's Indian Expedition During the Summer of 1863 and Record of the Troops Employed (Minneapolis, 1980), p. 23-25.

[50] Arthur Daniels, A Journal of Sibley's Indian Expedition During the Summer of 1863 and Record of the Troops Employed (Minneapolis, 1980), p. 25.

[51] Colonel William R. Marshall, Journal of the Military Expedition Against the Sioux Indians from Camp Pope in the Summer of 1863 Under Command of Brigadier General Henry Hastings Sibley (Original journal at the Minnesota Historical Society).

[52] Pritchett, John Perry. "On the march with Sibley in 1863: The Diary of Private Henry J. Hagadorn." North Dakota Historical Quarterly (Jan 1931), p. 120.

[54] Oscar Garrett Wall, Recollections of the Sioux Massacre (Lake City, MN, 1908), p. 258.

[55] Arthur Daniels, A Journal of Sibley's Indian Expedition During the Summer of 1863 and Record of the Troops Employed (Minneapolis, 1980), p. 26-27.

[56] Oscar Garrett Wall, Recollections of the Sioux Massacre (Lake City, MN, 1908), p. 258.

[57] Arthur Daniels, A Journal of Sibley's Indian Expedition During the Summer of 1863 and Record of the Troops Employed (Minneapolis, 1980), p. 28.

[58] Oscar Garrett Wall, Recollections of the Sioux Massacre (Lake City, MN, 1908), p. 259.

[59] Arthur Daniels, A Journal of Sibley's Indian Expedition During the Summer of 1863 and Record of the Troops Employed (Minneapolis, 1980), p. 29-30.

[60] Oscar Garrett Wall, Recollections of the Sioux Massacre (Lake City, MN, 1908), p. 259-60.

[61] Arthur Daniels, A Journal of Sibley's Indian Expedition During the Summer of 1863 and Record of the Troops Employed (Minneapolis, 1980), p. 30.

[62] Kaye L. Roehrick, N. Jane Hunt and Tom Kakonis, Brevet's North Dakota Historical Markers and Sites (Sioux Falls, SD: Brevet Press, Inc., 1975), p. 10.

[63] Arthur Daniels, A Journal of Sibley's Indian Expedition During the Summer of 1863 and Record of the Troops Employe (Minneapolis,

1980), p. 31-32.
[64] Oscar Garrett Wall,Recollections of the Sioux Massacre (Lake City, MN, 1908), p. 260.
[65] Arthur Daniels, A Journal of Sibley's Indian Expedition During the Summer of 1863 and Record of the Troops Employed (Minneapolis, 1980), p. 31-32.
[66] Colonel William R. Marshall, Journal of the Military Expedition Against the Sioux Indians from Camp Pope in the Summer of 1863 Under Command of Brigadier General Henry Hastings Sibley (Original journal at the Minnesota Historical Society).
[67] Arthur Daniels, A Journal of Sibley's Indian Expedition During the Summer of 1863 and Record of the Troops Employed (Minneapolis, 1980), p. 33-34.
[68] Oscar Garrett Wall, Recollections of the Sioux Massacre (Lake City, MN, 1908), p. 262.
[69] Oscar Garrett Wall, Recollections of the Sioux Massacre (Lake City, MN, 1908), p. 262-63.
[70] Colonel William R. Marshall, Journal of the Military Expedition Against the Sioux Indians from Camp Pope in the Summer of 1863 Under Command of Brigadier General Henry Hastings Sibley (Original journal at the Minnesota Historical Society).
[71] "Big Mound North Dakota: American Civil War July 24-25 1863." n.d. <http://www.americancivilwar.com/statepic/nd/nd001.html> (26 Jan. 2001).
[72] Arthur Daniels, A Journal of Sibley's Indian Expedition During the Summer of 1863 and Record of the Troops Employed (Minneapolis, 1980),

p. 36.
[73] Colonel William R. Marshall, Journal of the Military Expedition Against the Sioux Indians from Camp Pope in the Summer of 1863 Under Command of Brigadier General Henry Hastings Sibley (Original journal at the Minnesota Historical Society).
[74] Arthur Daniels, A Journal of Sibley's Indian Expedition During the Summer of 1863 and Record of the Troops Employed (Minneapolis, 1980), p. 37.
[75] Oscar Garrett Wall, Recollections of the Sioux Massacre (Lake City, MN, 1908), p. 263.
[76] Arthur Daniels, A Journal of Sibley's Indian Expedition During the Summer of 1863 and Record of the Troops Employe (Minneapolis, 1980), p. 37.
[77] Arthur Daniels, A Journal of Sibley's Indian Expedition During the Summer of 1863 and Record of the Troops Employed (Minneapolis, 1980), p. 37-40.
[78] Oscar Garrett Wall, Recollections of the Sioux Massacre (Lake City, MN, 1908), p. 269-70.
[79] "Dead Buffalo Lake North Dakota: American Civil War July 26, 1863." n.d. <http://www.americancivilwar.com/statepic/nd/nd002.html> (26 Jan. 2001).
[80] Oscar Garrett Wall, Recollections of the Sioux Massacre (Lake City, MN, 1908), p. 270.
[81] Arthur Daniels, A Journal of Sibley's Indian Expedition During the Summer of 1863 and Record of the Troops Employed (Minneapolis, 1980), p. 40.

82 Arthur Daniels, A Journal of Sibley's Indian Expedition During the Summer of 1863 and Record of the Troops Employed (Minneapolis, 1980), p. 40-42.

83 "Stony Lake North Dakota: American Civil War July 28, 1863." n.d. <http://www.americancivilwar.com/statepic/nd/nd003.html> (26 Jan. 2001).

84 Arthur Daniels, A Journal of Sibley's Indian Expedition During the Summer of 1863 and Record of the Troops Employed (Minneapolis, 1980) p. 42.

85 Colonel William R. Marshall, Journal of the Military Expedition Against the Sioux Indians from Camp Pope in the Summer of 1863 Under Command of Brigadier General Henry Hastings Sibley (Original journal at the Minnesota Historical Society).

86 H. A. Soule, "Early History of Sargent County." Cogswell Enterprise Feb. 19, 1925, p. 1.

87 Oscar Garrett Wall, Recollections of the Sioux Massacre (Lake City, MN, 1980) p. 274.

89 Oscar Garrett Wall, Recollections of the Sioux Massacre (Lake City, MN, 1908), p. 274-75.

90 Kaye L. Roehrick, N. Jane Hunt and Tom Kakonis, Brevet's North Dakota Historical Markers and Sites (Sioux Falls, SD:Brevet Press, Inc., 1975), p. 60.

91 Colonel William R. Marshall, Journal of the Military Expedition Against the Sioux Indians from Camp Pope in the Summer of 1863 Under Command of Brigadier General Henry Hastings Sibley (Original journal at the Minnesota Historical Society).

92 Arthur Daniels, A Journal of Sibley's Indian Expedition During the Summer of 1863 and Record of the Troops Employed (Minneapolis, 1980), p. 50.

93 Oscar Garrett Wall, Recollections of the Sioux Massacre (Lake City, MN, 1908), p. 276.

94 Arthur Daniels, A Journal of Sibley's Indian Expedition During the Summer of 1863 and Record of the Troops Employed (Minneapolis, 1980), p. 50.

95 Oscar Garrett Wall, Recollections of the Sioux Massacre (Lake City, MN, 1908), p. 277.

96 Arthur Daniels, A Journal of Sibley's Indian Expedition During the Summer of 1863 and Record of the Troops Employed (Minneapolis, 1980), p. 50.

97 Oscar Garrett Wall, Recollections of the Sioux Massacre (Lake City, MN, 1908), p. 277.

98 Arthur Daniels, A Journal of Sibley's Indian Expedition During the Summer of 1863 and Record of the Troops Employed (Minneapolis, 1980), p. 51-52.

99 Arthur Daniels, A Journal of Sibley's Indian Expedition During the Summer of 1863 and Record of the Troops Employed (Minneapolis, 1980), p. 52-54.

100 Oscar Garrett Wall, Recollections of the Sioux Massacre (Lake City, MN, 1908), p. 277-79.

101 Arthur Daniels, A Journal of Sibley's Indian Expedition During the Summer of 1863 and Record of the Troops Employed (Minneapolis, 1980), p. 55.

102 Stirum: Diamond Jubilee 1907-1982 (Stirum, ND, 1982), p. 1.

[103] Oscar Garrett Wall, <u>Recollections of the Sioux Massacre</u> (Lake City, MN, 1908), p. 280-81.

[104] Arthur Daniels, <u>A Journal of Sibley's Indian Expedition During the Summer of 1863 and Record of the Troops Employed</u> (Minneapolis, 1980), p. 55-58.

[105] Arthur Daniels, <u>A Journal of Sibley's Indian Expedition During the Summer of 1863 and Record of the Troops Employed</u> (Minneapolis, 1980), p. 58.

[106] Pritchett, John Perry. "On the March with Sibley in 1863: The Diary of Private Henry J. Hagadorn." <u>North Dakota Historical Quarterly</u> (Jan. 1931), p. 127.

[107] Arthur Daniels, <u>A Journal of Sibley's Indian Expedition During the Summer of 1863 and Record of the Troops Employed</u> (Minneapolis, 1980), p. 59-60.

[108] Arthur Daniels, <u>A Journal of Sibley's Indian Expedition During the Summer of 1863 and Record of the Troops Employed</u> (Minneapolis, 1980), p. 59-60.

Sibley Expedition Camps

1. Camp Pope	Headquarters	
2. Camp Crooks	June 16, 1863	
3. Camp Miller	June 17	
4. Camp Baker	June 18-19	
5. Camp McPhail	June 20-21	
6. Camp Ramsey	June 22	
7. Camp Averill	June 23	
8. Camp Marshall	June 24	
9. Camp Jennison	June 25	
10. Camp McLaren	June 26, 27, 28, 29	Present day Browns Valley, MN
11. Camp Bradley	June 30	
12. Camp Cook	July 1	
13. Camp Parker	July 2	East side of Lake Tewaukon, ND
14. Camp Buell	July 3	Present day Milnor, ND
15. Camp Hayes	July 4- July 10	Waited for attachment that went to Ft. Abercrombie from Camp McLaren
16. Camp Wharton	July 11-12	
17. Camp Weiser	July 13	
18. Camp Sheardown	July 14	
19. Camp Smith	July 15	
20. Camp Corning	July 16	
21. Camp Pope	July 17	
22. Camp Atchison	July 18- Aug. 11	Main Camp
23. Camp Forbes	July 20	
24. Camp Olin	July 21	
25. Camp Kimball	July 22	
26. Camp Grant	July 23	
27. Camp Sibley	July 24	Battle of Big Mound
28. Camp Whitney	July 25	
29. Camp Pfaener	July 26	Dead Buffalo Lake

30.	Camp Schoeneman	July 27	Stony Lake
31.	Camp Stees	July 28	On the Missouri River
32.	Camp Slaughter	July 29, 30, 31	
33.	Camp Braden	August 1	
34.	Camp Banks	August 2	
35.	Camp Kennedy	August 3	
36.	Camp Williston	August 4, 5	
37.	Camp Gilfillan	August 6	
38.	Camp Hall	August 7	
39.	Camp Carter	August 8, 9	
		August 10	Back to Camp Atchison
40.	Camp Burt	August 13	Return trip
41.	Camp Libby	August 14	
42.	Camp Arnold	August 15	
43.	Camp Stevens	August 16, 17	
44.	Camp Ambler	August 18	
45.	Camp Chase	August 19	
46.	Camp Edgerton	August 20	
47.	Camp Hacket	August 21, 22,	
		23, 24	Fort Abercrombie
48.	Camp Phelps	August 25	
49.	Camp White	August 26	
50.	Camp Heath	August 27	Near Pomme de Terre
51.	Camp Sullivan	August 28	
52.	Camp O'Connor	August 29, 30	
53.	Camp Jones	August 31	Westport, MN
54.	Camp Beever	September 1	
55.	Camp Rubles	September 2, 3	
56.	Camp Wilson	September 4	
57.	Camp Austin	September 5, 6	
58.	Camp Taylor	September 7	
59.	Camp Daniels	September 8	
60.	Camp Anderson	September 9	
61.	Camp Davys	September 10	
62.	Camp Rice	September 11	
63.	Camp Steele	September 12	Fort Snelling

Expedition 939 miles
From Fort Snelling to Fort Snelling 1059 miles

Interesting Facts
About the Sibley Expedition

* Two African Americans were on the Sibley Expedition. They were some of the first African Americans in North Dakota who were part of a military expedition.[1]

* "Several soldiers who took part in General Sibley's expedition were Norwegians and they suffered so much from mosquitoes, thirst and tiresome traveling through the rough prairies of Dakota that they received a very poor impression of the country." This discouraged many settlers from coming to North Dakota in the late 1800's.[2]

* There are no historical markers commemorating the Sibley Expedition in South Dakota or Minnesota.

* Four thousand seventy-five men with a large herd of beef cattle, and several hundred horses and mules traveled nine hundred thirty-nine miles over unbroken prairie in a little less than three months.[3]

* Due to the lack of wood the men burnt buffalo chips for warmth and fuel.[4]

* Most of the Indians that the men fought in battles, chased and even killed were not the Indians in Mankato, Minnesota at the time of the Uprising of 1862.

* When Lieutenant Frederick J. H. Beever was killed by the Indians on August 29, 1863, he was given what is believed to be the first Masonic burial in what is now North Dakota. Lieutenant John C. Whipple of the expedition was placed in charge of the funeral. The Lieutenants body was later re-buried in Oakland Cemetery in St. Paul.[5]

---

[1] Thomas P. Newgard, William C. Sherman, and John Guerrero, <u>African Americans in North Dakota: Sources and Assessments</u> (Bismarck,ND, 1994), p. 32.
[2] O. G. Libby, editor, <u>Collections of The State Historical Society</u> (Grand Forks, ND, 1925), p. 133.

[3] Oscar Garrett Wall, 'Recollections of the Sioux Massacre (Lake City, MN, 1908), p. 242-45.

[4] Colonel William R. Marshall, Journal of the Military Expedition Against the Sioux Indians from Camp Pope in the Summer of 1863 Under Command of Brigadier General Henry Hastings Sibley (Original journal at the Minnesota Historical Society)

[5] "Lt. Beever." n.d. <http://www.falmr.org/lt_beever.html> (20 September 2002)

Sibley Expedition campsites
throughout Minnesota

Camp Pope (Renville County) In or near Fort Ridgley, Minnesota. Named for the department commander General John Pope.

Camp Crooks (Renville County) Campsite used June 16, 1863. Eight miles northwest of Fort Ridgley, near the Minnesota River. It was named for Colonel William Crooks of the Sixth Minnesota.

Camp Miller (Renville County) Campsite used 17, 1863. The Wood Lake Battleground.

Camp Baker (Chippewa County) Campsite used June 18-19, 1863. On Red Iron Creek. It was named for Colonel James H. Baker of the 10th Minnesota.

Camp McPhail (Chippewa County) Campsite used June 20-21, 1863. Near the Minnesota River. It was named for Colonel Samuel McPhail of the First Minnesota Cavalry or Mounted Rangers.

Camp Ramsey (Swift County) Campsite used June 22, 1863. On a filthy green pond.

Camp Averill (Big Stone County) Campsite used June 23, 1863. Named for Lieutenant Colonel John T. Averill of the Sixth Minnesota.

Camp Marshall (Big Stone County) Campsite used June 24, 1863. Close to Big Stone Lake. Named for Lieutenant Colonel William R. Marshall of the Seventh Minnesota.

Camp Jennison (Big Stone County) Campsite used June 25, 1863. On Swan Lake. It was located on the southwest quarter of section twenty-five, township 123, range 49, between Big Stone Lake and the northeast shore of Bull Head. It was named for Lieutenant Colonel Samuel P. Jennison of the Tenth Minnesota.

Camp McLaren (Traverse County) Campsite used June 26-29, 1863. Between Big Stone Lake and Lake Traverse. Present-day Browns Valley, Minnesota. Named for Major Robert N. McLaren of the Sixth Minnesota.

South Dakota Campsites

Camp Bradley Campsite used June 30, 1863. It was probably located in the "northwest corner of township 126, range 50, in what is now Roberts County." It was named for Lieutenant Colonel George Bradley of the Seventh Minnesota.

Camp Cook Campsite used July 1, 1863. Sixteen miles from previous camp. It was located on the northwest quarter of section two, township 128, range 52. "Camp was made on the north shore of a shallow, treeless lake."

Sibley Expedition campsites throughout North Dakota

Camp Parker (Sargent County) Campsite used July 2, 1863. It was located on the "east end of Lake Tewaukon in SW 1/4 Section 32-129-53, Marboe Township, and named for Major John H. Parker of the First Minnesota Mounted Rangers."

Camp Buell (Sargent County) Campsite used July 3, 1863. Today this campsite is marked as a historic site. It is located on the south shore of Storm Lake in "Section 9-132-54, Milnor Township." "It was named for Major Salmon E. Buell of the First Regiment Minnesota Mounted Rangers, who would be a hero at the Battle of Big Mound on July 24, 1863."

Camp Hayes (Ransom County) Campsite used July 4-10, 1863. It was "named for Major Oren T. Hayes of the First Regiment Minnesota Mounted Rangers." "It was located in South 1/2 Section 36-134-55, Big Bend Township, eight miles southeast of Lisbon."

Camp Wharton (Ransom County) Campsite used July 11-12, 1863. It was "named for Dr. Alfred Wharton of the Sixth Minnesota Volunteer Infantry." It was located in "Section 19-135-56, Tuller Township", about five miles northwest of Lisbon."

Camp Weiser (Barnes County) Campsite used July 13, 1863. "Named for Dr. Joseph H. Weiser, Surgeon with the First Minnesota Mounted Rangers. He was later killed at the Battle of Big Mound." The site was located in the "north 1/2 Section 33-137-57, Thordenskjold Township, about four miles southwest of Nome. This site is part of the Storhoff farm off Highway 46. It is four miles west of the Nome Junction/Highway 32 Junction.

Camp Sheardown (Barnes County) Campsite used July 14, 1863. "Named for Dr. Samuel B. Sheardown of the Tenth Minnesota Infantry. Located in northwest 1/4 Sec. 2-139-58, Marsh Township, about three miles south of present day Valley City, the site is today marked by a bronze tablet." From Valley City, south .1 mile from I-94 exit #294 to frontage road, west .5 mile on asphalt road, south 1.25 miles on 118 Avenue SE (a gravel road). The bronze tablet is just after the turn in the gravel road.

Camp Smith (Barnes County) Campsite used July 15, 1863. "Named for Dr. Lucius B. Smith, Surgeon of the 7th Regiment. Located in west 1/2 Section 30-131-57, Noltimier Township, six miles northeast of Valley City."

Camp Corning (Barnes County) Campsite used July 16, 1863. "It was located in southeast 1/4 Section 7-143-58, Sibley Township, about seven miles northeast of Dazey. A granite monument marks the site, which is named for Captain Edward Corning, Quartermaster to Sibley's staff. The site is at the corner of the turn to Sibley Crossing on Barnes County 19, a gravel road."

Camp Pope (Griggs County) Campsite used July 17,1863. "It was located in northwest 1/4 Section 4-145-59, Ball Hill Township, five miles east of Sutton and named for Captain Douglas Pope of General Sibley's staff. Six hundred seventy-six men were encamped here. Captain Pope later married Augusta Sibley, the Generals eldest daughter."

Camp Atchison (Griggs County) Campsite used July 18, 1863. "Located on the northeast shore of Lake Sibley in Section 29-147-60, Addie Township, four miles south of Binford. It was named for Captain Charles B. Atchison, an aide of Major General John Pope, who was on temporary assignment to General Sibley. Atchison joined the army in 1861 in his native Illinois, and served until his death on May 10, 1876." Today this site is a state historic site. The site is nine miles east of Cooperstown on Highway 200 and then five miles north on Highway 1. At Camp Atchison, two men died. George E. Brent, Company D, 1st Minnesota Mounted Rangers, was accidentally shot on July 20th and was buried on a high hill southwest of camp. A few weeks later on August 9th, Samuel Wannamaker, Company E, 10th Minnesota Infantry, died of sickness and was buried outside the north edge of camp.

Camp Forbes (Foster County) Campsite used July 20, 1863. "Named for Captain William H. H. Forbes." The site is located in southwest 1/4 Section 33-146-63, Rolling Prairie Township, and is about six miles south of Juanita.

Camp Olin (Foster County) Campsite used July 21, 1863. "Named for Captain Rolin C. Olin, who had been a 2nd Lieutenant in the 3rd Minnesota Infantry. He was captured by the Confederates on July 19, 1862, and formally exchanged and released. He was promoted to Captain May 11, 1863, and assigned to General Sibley's staff. The site in Section 33-145-64, Buchephalia Township, is about midway between Kensal and Bordulac."

Camp Kimball (Foster County) Campsite used July 22, 1863. It could have been named for "Surgeon General James P. Kimball of Fort Buford or for Captain William H. Kimball, Assistant

Quartermaster for General Sibley." The site is located in Section 16-145-67, Longview Township. Today this site is a state historic site and is five miles southwest of Carrington.

Camp Grant (Stutsman County) Campsite used July 23, 1863. Located in "southwest 1/4 Section 24-143-69, Gerber Township, five miles northwest of Woodworth and named for Captain Hiram P. Grant of the expedition." Today this site is a historic site.

Camp Sibley (Kidder County) Campsite used July 24, 1863. Named for General Sibley. The exact site is not known. It was "on the bank of a large lake, possibly Kunkel Lake in Buckeye Township (141-71). It was near this camp that the Battle of Big Mound took place and where Dr. Weiser was killed. The Adjacent township is named for Dr. Weiser. Their events are commemorated at the Burman Historic Site in northwest 1/4 Section 24-141-71, on a parcel of land donated by John Burman, who homesteaded here in 1906."

Camp Whitney (Kidder County) Campsite used July 25, 1863. Named for Captain Joseph C. Whitney. The exact spot of this campsite is unknown. It is thought to be "about eight miles north of Tappen in Westford Township (140-71). In 1951 John DeKrey Jr. donated a three acre plot in northwest 1/4 Section 5-140-71, known today as the McPhail Butte Historic Site."

Camp Pfaender (Kidder County) Campsite used July 26, 1863. Thought to be located on the south shore of Dead Buffalo Lake in "Section 33-140-72, Vernon Township, two miles northwest of Dawson. The origin of the name Pfaender is unknown." All other Sibley campsites are named for senior officers on the expedition.

Camp Schoenemann (Burleigh County) Campsite used July 27, 1863. The exact site is unknown, but it was "probably located near southeast 1/4 Section 18-139-75, Driscoll Township, two miles west of Driscoll, the site of Driscoll Sibley Park. The Battle of Stony Lake was fought the following day about one mile northeast of the campsite." The camp was named for Captain Rudolph Schoenemann.

Camp Stees (Burleigh County) Campsite used July 28, 1863. It was named for Captain Charles J. Stees. The exact location is unknown but is was probably "about eighteen miles from Camp Schoenemann on the banks of Apple Creek, most likely about two miles northwest of Menoken in Menoken Township."

Camp Slaughter (Burleigh County) Campsite used July 29, 30, 31. This campsite marked the end of the Sibley Expedition. On August 1, the Expedition began its return mark to Fort Snelling, MN. The camp was named for Captain Thomas I. Slaughter. This site was "just above the mouth of Apple Creek, in Section 28-138-80, Lincoln Township, four miles south of Bismarck, at what was then named Burned Boat Island from an incident during the 1834 visit of Prince Maximilian of Wied. It is now renamed Sibley Island, and is a popular picnic grounds."

Camp Braden (Burleigh County) Campsite used August 1, 1863. This was the first campsite on Sibley's return march. It was named for Captain William W. Braden. "It was probably just northeast of present-day Menoken in Menoken Township (139-78)."

Camp Banks (Burleigh County) Campsite used August 2, 1863. It was named for Captain Rolla Banks. This site was "just beyond the earlier Camp Schoenemann, probably three miles north of Driscoll in Driscoll Township (139-75)." At this campsite, the Indian scout Chaska died suddenly during the night and was buried near the camp. "He is memorialized by the so-called Camp Chaska Historical Site in southwest 1/4 Section 34-140-75, Clear Lake Township, just to the north of the probable site of Camp Banks."

Camp Kennedy (Kidder County) Campsite used August 3, 1863. It was named for Captain John Kennedy. The exact spot of this campsite is unknown however, it was probably in Vernon Township (140-72), about ten miles northeast of Steele.

Camp Williston (Kidder County) Campsite used August 4 and 5, 1863. It was named for Captain William C. Williston. This camp was located on the "same lake, but not the same site, as Camp Sibley, used eleven days earlier." The exact site is unknown but it was probably "on Kunkel Lake in Buckeye Township (141-71).

Camp Gilfillan (Stutsman County) Campsite used August 6, 1863. It was named for Captain James Gilfillan. The camp was "located in southwest 1/4 Section 13-143-68, Wadsworth Township, six miles northeast of Woodworth."

Camp Hall (Foster County) Campsite used August 7, 1863. It was named for Captain Thomas G. Hall. The site was located in "Section 24-145-66, Melville Township, about midway between Melville and Bordulac."

Camp Carter (Foster County) Campsite used August 8 and 9, 1863. It was named for Captain Theo. G. Carter. The site was "located in Section 2-145-64, Bucephalia Township, eleven miles south of Grace City."

Camp Burt (Griggs County) Campsite used August 13, 1863. From the 10th to the 12th the Expedition was at their main camp, Camp Atchison. This campsite was used on their return journey to Fort Abercrombie. It was named for Captain William H. Burt. The site was "located in northeast 1/4 Section 35-145-59, Ball Hill Township, two miles north east of Hannaford."

Camp Libby (Barnes County) Campsite used August 14, 1863. It was named for Captain Asa Libby Jr. The site was "located in southwest 1/4 Section 13-142-58, Ashtabula Township, fourteen miles north north-east of Valley City."

Camp Arnold (Barnes County) Campsite used August 15, 1863. It was named for Captain John K. Arnold. The site was "located in Section 34-141-56, Weimer Township, four miles north of Oriska. On June 25, 1933, a historical site was dedicated although it was in northeast 1/4 Section 32-141-56, two miles west of the actual camp."

Camp Stevens (Cass County) Campsite used August 16-17, 1863. It was named for Captain Albert H. Stevens. The site was "located in southeast 1/4 Section 2-139-55, Hill Township, six miles southeast of Tower City on the east bank of the Maple River."

Camp Ambler (Cass County) Campsite used August 18, 1863. It was named for Captain Rufus C. Ambler. The site was "located in northwest 1/4 Section 36-138-53, Walburg Township, six miles northwest of Leonard." It was located near the Maple River. "A plot of land for a historic site was donated by owner Alvin Zaeske."

Camp Chase (Richland County) Campsite used August 19, 1863. It was named for Captain Jonah Chase. The exact location of the site is unknown, however it was probably "located in the northeast part of Barrie Township (136-51), just south west of Kindred on the banks of the Sheyenne River."

Camp Edgerton (Richland County) Campsite used August 20, 1863. It was named for Captain Alonzo J. Edgerton. The exact spot is unknown, but "it was one day's march from Fort Abercrombie, probably in Walcott Township, just northwest of present-day Walcott."

Camp Hackett (Richland County) Campsite used August 21-24 1863. This camp was located in or just near Fort Abercrombie, in "Section 4-134-38, Abercrombie Township. It was named for Captain Charles W. Hackett. This was the last campsite in what is now North Dakota. The Expedition left here on August 25 and arrived at Fort Snelling, MN on September 12, 1863."

Detachment Campsites

Camp Libby (Richland) "This was the first campsite used by the detachment of soldiers that left Fort Abercrombie on July 6, 1863, to join the main column of the Sibley Expedition at Camp Hayes, about fifty-six miles to the west." It was named for Captain Asa Libby Jr. This site was located "about five miles west of the fort, [Fort Abercrombie] just across the Wild Rice River, probably in Abercrombie Township (134-49)."

Camp Tattersall (Richland County) The second campsite used by the detachment on its way to Camp Hayes. Campsite used July 7, 1863. It was named in honor of Captain William K. Tattersall. The site was "probably located in Freeman Township (134-52), about ten miles northwest of Wyndmere."

Camp Wilson (Ranson County) This was the third and last campsite used by the detachment on its way to Camp Hayes. Campsite used July 8, 1863. It was named in honor Captain Eugene M. Wilson. This site was located only a "few miles east of Camp Hayes, probably in Scoville Township (134-54), on the west bank of the Sheyenne River about ten miles east southeast of Lisbon."

Camp Rusten (Griggs County) This was a camp used by Colonel McPhail detachment. This detachment split from Sibley's main column and headed southward west of the Sheyenne. This site was "located in Section 23-145-60, Helena Township, three miles southeast of Sutton. The origin of the name is unknown."

Minnesota Campsites

Camp Phelps (Wilkin County) Campsite used August 25, 1863. Eleven miles down Red River from Fort Abercrombie. Near Breckenridge, Minnesota. Named for Captain William W. Phelps of the Tenth Minnesota.

Camp White (Grant County) Campsite used August 26, 1863. In Grant County Minnesota, near the Otter Tail River. Named for Captain George T. White of the Tenth Minnesota.

Camp Heath (Grant County) Campsite used August 27, 1863. Near Pomme de Terre River and Lake. A few miles east of Elbow Lake. Located in the vicinity of the Tipsinah Mounds Park and Campground. Named for Captain John W. Heath of the Tenth Minnesota.

Camp Sullivan (Douglas County) Campsite used August 28, 1863. Crossed the Pomme de Terre River. Eighteen miles southeast of Camp Heath. Named for Captain Michael H. Sullivan of the Ninth Minnesota.

Camp O'Connor (Douglas County) Campsite used August 29-30, 1863. East of Camp Sullivan fifteen miles. Named for Captain Michael J. O'Connor of the Ninth Minnesota.

Camp Jones (Douglas County) Campsite used August 31, 1863. East of Camp O'Connor. Named for Captain John Jones of the Third Minnesota Battery.

Camp Beever (Pope County) Campsite used September 1, 1863. On Jones Lake. Present-day Westport, Minnesota. Named for Lieutenant F. J. H. Beever.

Camp Rubles (Stearns County) Campsite used September 2-3, 1863. Sauk Centre. Named for Captain George S. Ruble of the Minnesota Mounted Rangers.

Camp Wilson (Stearns County) Campsite used September 4, 1863. Eighteen and a half miles east of Sauk Centre. Named for Captain Eugene M. Wilson of the First Regiment Minnesota Mounted Rangers.

Camp Austin (Stearns County) Campsite used September 5-6, 1863. Sixteen miles east of Camp Wilson. Named for Captain Horace Austin of the First Minnesota Mounted Rangers.

Camp Taylor (Stearns County) Campsite used September 7, 1863. Two and a half miles west of Saint Cloud, Minnesota. Named for Captain Oscar Taylor of the First Regiment Minnesota Mounted Rangers.

Camp Daniels (Sherburne County) Campsite used September 8, 1863. Six and a half miles east of Saint Cloud. Named for Captain Joseph Daniels of the Minnesota Mounted Rangers.

Camp Anderson (Sherburne County) Campsite used September 9, 1863. On Big Lake. Named for Captain Joseph Anderson of the Minnesota Mounted Rangers.

Camp Davys (Anoka County) Campsite used September 10, 1863. On high ground near Anoka, Minnesota. Four miles from St. Anthony (present-day Minneapolis). Named for Captain Peter B. Davy of the Minnesota Mounted Rangers.

Camp Rice (Hennepin County) Campsite used September 11, 1863. Sixteen miles west of Fort Snelling.

Camp Steele (Ramsey County) Campsite used September 12, 1863. In or near Fort Snelling.

North Dakota campsites information obtained from:
Douglas A. Wick, *North Dakota Place Names* (Bismarck, ND: Hedemarken Collectibles, 1988) ;and from the authors own observations of the trail.

Minnesota campsites obtained from:
Arthur M. Daniels, *A Journal of Sibley's Indian Expedition During the Summer of 1863 and Record of the Troops Employed* (Minneapolis, MN: James D. Thueson, 1980) and from the authors own observations of the trail.

South Dakota campsites and Camp Jennison, Minnesota campsite obtained from:
Dana Wright, "The Sibley Trail In North Dakota," *North Dakota Historical Quarterly* vol. I. (April 1927): 30-45.

Standing Buffalo

Standing Buffalo (Tatanka Nazin) was "the chief of a band of Sissetons whose village was on the shores of Big Stone Lake." During the time of the Yellow Medicine incident, as the Indians were starving, Standing Buffalo still believed in the whites. Other Indians favored violent retaliation, but Standing Buffalo did not. A council was formed to determine what should be done, Standing Buffalo was part of this council. The council voted in favor of resorting to arms to right the wrongs done to them. At this time, Standing Buffalo went to the troops headquarters and to tell the troops what the council had decided. He told the soldiers that he had come to warn them and that they should be prepared and on alert. Throughout the Massacre Standing Buffalo, as well as he could, kept his people out of it. When General Sibley demanded that Little Crow surrender all his white prisoners unconditionally, Standing Buffalo was on the council that would determine what should be done. He said that he believed that the whites should be delivered unharmed. He also said that he believed that the Lower Indians had caused him and his people great harm, because neither he nor his people had killed any whites, but they have had to suffer for what the Lower Indians did. Standing Buffalo and his people were present at the Battle of Big Mound and were probably forced to fight the whites, to safeguard themselves and their families.

Years after the Sibley Expedition on June 5, 1871, Standing Buffalo was "solicited by the Yanktons to join them in a raid on the Gros Ventres and Upper Assiniboines." He urged them not to attack and said that it would anger the whites. The Yanktons then accused him of having regard for the whites which would make him unworthy of his chieftainship. Standing Buffalo was tired of the years of hardship and of arguing with fellow Indians. He resolved to join in the fight and finally end it all. During the battle that followed, he led a charge into a group of superior forces, never firing a shot. "He fell from his horse in the midst of the enemy, his body pierced with upwards of thirty bullets."

– From; Recollections of the Sioux Massacre by Oscar Garrett Wall, (Lake City, MN, 1908), p. 177-182.

Little Crow

Little Crow was a Sioux chief, but was "not especially loved by his people, who regarded him as a tyrant." One reason why he was feared by his people was that earlier in his life he had fought with his brothers and murdered two of them. "In his violent encounters both of his arms were broken, and Indian surgery had not so reduced the fractures as to prevent deformity in the appearance of his arms when those members were exposed to view." Due to his deformity, he was able to be identified when he was killed.

As well, Little Crow was a skilled warrior and excelled in the art of gambling, a pastime engaged in by many Indians. Another noted feature of Little Crow was, "that his front teeth, above and below, were double." To Little Crow's honor, he did protest against the killing of women and children, which he saw as wrong and cowardly.

– From; Recollections of the Sioux Massacre by Oscar Garrett Wall (Lake City, MN, 1908), p. 183-186.

Little Crows Death

Nathan Lampson in the company of his son, Chauncey, killed Little Crow on the evening of July 3, 1863, near Hutchinson, Minnesota. During the spring and summer of 1863, the Lampson family, along with many others lived in the Hutchinson stockade for safety. Nathan and his son Chauncey, however spent most of their time looking after their farm, six miles north of Hutchinson. On the night of the 3rd, with food scare, Nathan and his son, set out to find and kill a deer. As they were out, they spotted two Indians picking wild raspberries. Nathan shot at Little Crow, with the bullet passing just above Little Crow's hip. Little Crow then went down but regained his footing and both Little Crow and his son went after Nathan and Chauncey. Chauncey and Little Crow then met and both fired at one another, Chauncey's bullet killed Little Crow. The next morning, a team was sent out and the body of an Indian was recovered, it was later recognized as that of Little Crow.

– From; Recollections of the Sioux Massacre by Oscar Garrett Wall (Lake City, MN, 1908), p. 187-190.

List of Casualties

- *Dr. Josiah S. Weiser*, 1st Minnesota Mounted Rangers, murdered by Indians Friday afternoon, July 24th, 1863, at Camp Sibley. Today a monument pays tribute to his death at the Burman Historic Site.

- *Lieut. Ambrose Freeman*, Co. D, 1st Minnesota Mounted Rangers, murdered by Indians Friday July 24th, 1863, near Camp Whitney.

- *Gustav A. Stark*, Co. B. Rangers, killed July 24th during the Battle of Big Mound.

- *Andrew Moore*, Co. B. Rangers, fatally wounded on August 15th at Camp Chase. He was buried four miles north of present day Oriska, North Dakota at Camp Arnold.

- *Corporal Wm. Haslip*, Co. B, Rangers, wounded in shoulder.

- *John Murphy*, Co. B, Rangers, killed by a stroke of lightning while charging on Indians during the Battle of Big Mound on July 24th.

- *John Platt*, Co. L, Rangers, wounded July 26th in a charge and died on Tuesday, July 28th, at Camp Stees.

- *Sergeant James Grady*, Co. L, Rangers, wounded.

- *Private Henry Stutz*, Co. B, Rangers, wounded.

- *George E. Brent*, Co. D, Rangers, shot himself at Camp Forbes on July 21st. He was buried on a high hill southwest of Camp Atchison.

- *Frederick J. H. Beever*, murdered by Indians on August 29th near Camp Slaughter.

- *Nicholas Miller*, Co. K, 6th Regiment, murdered by Indians August 29th, at Missouri River (Camp Slaughter).

- *Samuel Wannemaker*, Co. E, 10th, died of Fever at Camp Atchison. He was buried outside the north edge of camp.

- *Christian Peterson*, Co. D Cavalry, died of Fever August 13 near Camp Libby.

- *James Pontsford*, Co. D. Cavalry, died of Fever August 15. He was buried four miles north of present day Oriska, North Dakota at Camp Arnold.

- *Matthew L. Dearmin*, Co. E, 10th, died of Fever at Fort Abercrombie, August 22nd.

- *Edwin McMannis*, Co. F, Cavalry, died of Fever at Fort Abercrombie.

- *George Wood*, Co. F, Cavalry, died of Fever at Fort Abercrombie.

- *Richard D. Brower*, Co. D, Cavalry, died of Fever at Fort Abercrombie, September 6th.

Record of Troops

Brigadier General and Staff

H. H. Sibley, Brigadier General
     Date of Commission- 29 September, 1862
R. C. Olin, Assistant Adjt. General
     Date of Commission- 11 March, 1863
D. Pope, Captain and A.D.C.
     Date of Commission- 30 June, 1862
C. B. Atchison, Captain and A.D.C.
     Date of Commission- 11 July, 1862
F. H. Pratt, Lieut. and Vol. A.D.C.
     Date of Commission- 26 May, 1863
F. J. H. Beever, Lieut. and A.D.C.
     Date of Commission- Appointed June 15, 1863
S. C. Flandreau, Lieut. and Vol. A.D.C.
     Date of Commission- Appointed June 15, 1863
A. Hawthorne, Lieut. and Vol. A.D.C.
     Date of Commission- Appointed June 15, 1863
W. H. Forbes, Commissary of Subsistence
     Date of Commission- 9 November 1862
Edward Corning, Quartermaster
     Date of Commission- 24 March 1862
WM. Kimball, Quartermaster
     Date of Commission- 27 March, 1863

Chief Guides and Scouts

Guides
Pierre Bottineau
Joseph R. Brown

Sioux Interpreter
S. R. Riggs

Scouts
George A. McCloud
J. J. Duley

Ninth Regiment
Co. "A"

Mostly from St. Anthony- Acted as Pioneers

Captain Jonah Chase, November 20, 1862
1st Lieut. Harrison Jones, November 20, 1862
1st Sergeant Leon M. Lane, November 20
2nd Sergeant H. A. C. Thompson, August 14
3rd do David B. Ellis, August 14
*4th do Beverly C. Bonham, August 14
5th do Abner Spencer, November 20
1st Corporal Alfred S. Snow, August 14, 1862
2nd Corporal Charles Estes, August 14, 1862
3rd Charles Shoorod, August 14, 1862
4th Lewis C. Timpson, August 14, 1862
5th Daniel Hutchins, August 14, 1862
6th James A. Woodcock, August 14, 1862
7th-not on expedition
8th Vacancy

Musicians

Edward Warren   Wm. O'Brien

Privates

John Allen	Jas Leighton
Charles Bunell	Sam Merrill
Hiram Barnard	Sam Macomber
Robert A. Benson	John McCrimmon
Richmond Burrows	John McDougal
Alonzo Bragdon	James McCosh
*John B. Chase	Thomas May
Benj F. Cooley	John Pomeroy
Burton T. Cooley	Geo Pomeroy
*Tameron Campbell	John Peil
Charles A. Delvin	Stephen Rogerson
Amos Day	Chas Ricker
Jerry Desmond	*Joseph Richards
George Dorman	Henry Seeley
*Charles Farrow	Chas Spencer
James Fulerton	Jas Styles
*Frank Goodin	Warren Stetson
Louis Gamash	Hugh Smith
Benj F. Gray	*Mortimer Swingle
George Goodwin	Wm Stockton
Joseph Gould	Paul Shappee
*Tillson Heath	Geo Shappee
Charles Haven	James Sinclair
David Hewitt	Wm Todd
George Kenney	Geo Wetheren

Sixth Regiment, M.V.

Colonel William Crooks, Commissioned August 23, 1862.
Lieut. Col. John T. Averill, August 22.
Major Robert N. McLaren, August 22 -2nd Lt. Co., August 1st;
 Capt. August 18th.
Adjutant Florenton E. Snow, August 21.
Quartermaster Henry L. Carver, August 21, 1862.
Surgeon Alfred Wharton, August 21.
1st Ass't Jared W. Daniels, August 23.
2nd Ass't Augustus O. Potter, August 23.
Sergeant Major Frederic W. Norwood.
Com. Sergeant Wm. S. McCauley.
Q. M. Sergeant Henry D. Tenney.
Hospital Steward H. H. Gillis.
Principal Musicians Samuel D. Freeman, Simeon Farrington.

Company "A."

Organized August 18, 1862- From St. Paul.

Captain Hiram P. Grant, Commissioned August 12, 1862.
1st Lieut. Harry J. Gillham, August 18.
1st Sergeant Wm. Pratt, Appointed September 4, 1863.
2nd. Serg't Alonzo P. Connelly, September 4, 1863.
3rd Serg't Geo. W. Brannan, September 4, 1863.
4th Serg't Rasmus Olson, September 4, 1863.
5th Serg't George B. Gardner, September 4, 1863. Color Bearer.
1st Corporal W. T. Barnes, September 4, 1863.
3rd Corporal Melville B. Fields, September 4, 1863.
4th Corporal Seth Fielding, September 4, 1863.
6th Corporal Theodore Miller, September 4, 1863.
7th Corporal James Auge, September 4, 1863.
*8th Corporal Joseph Maddison, September 4, 1863.

Musician
Maurice Nealy

Wagoner
Alfred B. Shadduck

Bugler
Milton R. Seaman

Privates

Benj F. Arbuckle
Joseph Alord
Moses Bryant
Chas Bryant
Wm W. Bolton
Wm T. Barnes
Enoch Brown
Paul Brinnelle
Patrick H. Byrnes
*Joseph F. Chapron
Wm H. Caine
John Chalmers
Joseph Chadwick
Basile DeRosie
*Erick A. Erickson
Peter Felix
Dania Felix
Patrick Freany
Henry C. Greanlee
John Howard
Wm. Havens
*And G. Hilberge
*Joseph Havens
Sam Hart
Alvin Hayford
Hanke Johnson
Maller Johnson
Francis Jarvis
Aaron Jay
John R. King

Jas S. Leyde
Swan Linstron
Chas Lawson
Theodore Miller
Dan H. McCauley
Dennis Murphy
Horatio C. Marsden
Alex R. McCloud
Loais Malo
Alford Miller
Jeremiah McCarty
Geo Nimmo
Willard A. Newcombe
Wm H. Rossman
Wm Schuder
Chas W. Smith
Dennis Sweeny
James H. Slover
Wm H. Shafer
Francis Trepan
Peter F. Thielan
Marvin H. Tolan
Dan F. Terwilleger
Wm Vayhinger
Berhard Webber
Chas Weed
Lewis Walker
*John West
Richard White
Samuel J. Weiting
Ernst Wagner

Company "B."

Organized August 18, 1862 - From Minneapolis and Hennepin County.

1st Lieut. William Grant, August 8, 1862.
1st Serg't Francis H. Wheeler, Appointed August 19, 1862.
2nd Serg't William Moore, August 19, 1862.
*3rd Serg't Frank N. Fleming, August 19, 1862.
4th Serg't Levinne P. Plummer, August 19, 1862.
*5th Serg't Perez Benjamin, August 19, 1862.
1st Corporal Wm. P. C. Hank, August 19, 1862.
2nd. Corporal Edward R. Norris, August 19, 1862.
*3rd. Corporal Bela F. Burrill, August 19, 1862.

4th Corporal Leonard J. Young, August 19, 1862.
5th Corporal John Jacobs, August 19, 1862.
6th Corporal Thomas Hannay, August 19, 1862.
7th Corporal James Lafan, August 19, 1862.
8th Corporal Marcus Brownell, August 19, 1862.

Musicians
Alfred B. Robinson,   *James H. Jones

Wagoner
Francis G. Mitchell

Bugler
Levi Longfellow

Privates

Miles Allen
Simeon Auer
David Auge
Wm. Armstrong
Eben J. Brugdon
Henry Brewer
Wm. H. Bartlow
Wm. W. Birch
Orland H. Bushnell
James C. Brandon
Wm. Batdorf
Benj F. Colburn
Peter Church
Francis A. Clay
Geo H. Day
Marcus A. Denney
John L. Fleming
John Galbreath
Jonathan L. Grave
Chas F. Grave

Andrew Huff
Chas H. Hopper
Levi T. Hanson
*Lewis C. Johnson
Cyrus H. Jenks
*Chas H. Libby
Westley Lambert
Ennis N M'Gray
Parlane McFarlane
Elisha M. Murch
Jas McManus
Sam N. Pavitt
John A. Rank
David Ramsey
Dan S. Styner
Wm R. Sheppard
John D. Stufford
Silas Somers
And Thompson
Sam D. Thompson
John C. Vost

Company "C."

Organized August 12, 1862 - From Rice County.
[Remained at Camp Atchison]

1st Lieut. Dana L. White.
◊1st Sergeant Robert R. Hutchinson.
2nd Sergeant Edwin W. Dimmick.
5th Sergeant John Hutchinson.
2nd Corporal John W. Gould.
3rd Corporal Amasa Closson.

4th Corporal John F. McClintock.
5th Corporal Chas. M. Hetherington.
6th Corporal Ernest Lempf.
7th Corporal Samuel McClay.
8th Corporal Frank F. Hutchinson.

Musicians

Thomas Shipton

Alex M. Thompson

Wagoner
Aaron L. Corney

Bugler
Wm. E. Poe

Privates

Stephen Allen
John Barren
Myron Bates
Chester S. Boss
John Brown
Wm Burrows
Thos Barnes
Schuyler Closson
Lloyd D. Copeland
Louis Beerman
August Beerman
Geo Beerman
And Chapin
Sam Clarke
Benj F. Davison
Leonidas H. Dunin
◊Jas Emerson
Geo Fogg
Sylvester Glidden
Chas Grann
Jerry B. Jones

And Kahler
John Keller
John Logan
John Mourrer
John Merkel
John Malcolm
Chas Prince
John D. Plummer
Jas Rice
Wm Rumsey
Geo W. Robinson
John Richey
And R. Roberts
Cornelius Sullivan
John Stewart
Newell J. Sumner
Horace C. Stranahan
August Shollenberger
Theodore Sanderson
Dan B. Turner
Thos Talbot
Alex Thorp
Herbert M. Young
Jesse B. Young

Company "D."

Organized at Fort Snelling, August 15, 1862 - From Minneapolis.

Captain Joseph C. Whitney, Commissioned August 16, 1862.
1st Lieut. S. H. King, August 12, 1862.
◊1st Sergeant Wm. F. Atkinson, Appointed August 16, 1862.
3rd Sergeant George E. Case, Appointed August 16, 1862.
4th Sergeant Elijah Farrington, Appointed August 16, 1862.

5th Sergeant H. M. Huntington, Appointed August 16, 1862.
1st Corporal Henry Snyder, Appointed August 16, 1862.
3rd Corporal Reuben Robinson, Appointed August 16, 1862.
4th Corporal Washington Pierce, Appointed August 16, 1862.
5th Corporal Henry E. Selden, Appointed August 16, 1862.
6th Corporal Elias G. Brown, Appointed August 16, 1862.
7th Corporal John Wait, Appointed August 16, 1862.
8th Corporal John S. Day, Appointed August 16, 1862.

Musicians

George A. Cressey   Hannibal Hodsden

Wagoner
John F. Bell

Privates

Jas Allen
Geo Ames
Wm C. Brown
Jas W. Baird
Chas J. Beedy
Asa D. Brown
Frank S. Coffin
Francis M. Carman
Rob't B. Coffin
Sam W. Costellow
Geo E. Collins
*Henry Curtis
Mariner W. Cates
Nelson Dubuque
Edwin E. Edgerly
Enos W. Ellaman
Crocker P. Fletcher
Julius Farrington
Jas S. Foster
Austin L. Fenlason
Wm B. Franklin
Allen L. Goodrich
Chas E. Galpin
Albert F. Grove
Wm A Haukins
Frank J. Heiss
James Huntington
Geo A. Hill
Jas A. Harmin
*Edwin Jackson
*Chas W. Johnson
Jos A. James
*Isaiah H. Judd

Wm F. Kiekenapp
Silas Livingston
Chas B. Lansing
*Levi L. Leathers
Alfred Loftus
Andrew Layman
Wm W. Mills
John McKimball
Chas H. Moore
Bailey Madison
Wesley Neill
James Pratt
Eddie Powers
Dean R. Richardson
Isaiah Richardson
*Theodoric Ray
John M. Richardson
August Rohe
Aretas Smith
Albion Stinson
Wm R. Stinson
Oscar H. Shepley
John S. Stoops
Lewis Sanford
Sylvanus W. Stinson
Isaiah Thompson
Willard S. Whitmore
◊Chas H. Zimmermann

Company "E."

Organized August, 1862 - From St. Paul.

Captain Rudolph Schoenemann, Commissioned August 18, 1862.
2nd Lieut. Mathias Holl, August 23, 1862.
1st Serg't Justus B. Bell, August 18, 1862.
2nd Serg't George Huhn, August 18, 1862.
3rd Serg't Elias Siebert, August 18, 1862.
4th Serg't Paul P. Huth, August 18, 1862.
5th Serg't Mathias Miller, August 18, 1862.
1st Corporal William Rodhe
2nd Corporal Peter F. Leitner
3rd Corporal Reinhard Stiefel
4th Corporal George Sauer
5th Corporal Joseph Smith
6th Corporal Frederic Martin
7th Corporal Michael Nierburg
8th Corporal Joseph Eheim

Musicians
Wm. D. Sproesser *Charles Seidel

Wagoner
Henry Henricks

Privates

Wm Bast	Jacob Mann
Peter H. Beckendorf	Chas Metz
Ferd Besecker	John J. Miller
John Blesius	M. Muckenhausen
Michael Boos	John Munson
Christian Bristle	Thos A. C. Parks
Henry Detert	Geo Paulson
Chas Ebert	O. C. Peterson
Joseph Ferlein	Chas Plesner
Sam Gaheen	Antoine A. Praxel
Joseph Goldner	Rudolph Radke
Henry Grapel	August Rehse
Carl F. Hahn	John Reimer
Jacob Hauck	*Henry Reuter
Herman Heelman	Henry Schaefer
Fred Henricks	August Scheibel
Nicholas Hosheid	Wm Schene
*Conrad Jacobi	Geo Schermann
Jacob John	Fred Schoenheiter
Louis Jurgens	John Simon
August Kellerman	Wm A. Smith
Jacob Kernen	G. Steugelin
Phillip Killian	Chas Temme
◊Louis Klinkhammer	Louis Thiele
*Fred Kraemer	Louis Wetteran
Henry Krueger	August Williams
Wm Mahle	Jean Rossian

Company "F."

Organized August 18, 1862 - From Goodhue County.

1st Lieut. George W. Parker, August 22, 1862.
2nd Lieut. Joseph C. Pingrey, August 22, 1862.
1st Sergeant John J. Clagee, Appointed August 22, 1862.
2nd Serg't John Reimund, August 22, 1862.
3rd Serg't Ole Nelson, August 22, 1862.
*1st Corporal Charles W. Brink, August 22, 1862.
2nd Corporal Jos. A. Woodberry, August 22, 1862.
3rd Corporal Andrew J. Johnson, August 22, 1862.
4th Corporal Oliver W. Sprake, August 22, 1862.
5th Corporal Wm. H. Wellington, August 22, 1862.
6th Corporal H. N. Eggleston, August 22, 1862.
7th Corporal Wm. L. Kinney, August 22, 1862.

Musicians
*Rinaldo Godfrey   Allen Swain

Wagoner   **Bugler**
*Franklin H. Bullock   Daniel C. Smith

Privates

Robt N. Akers
Sam Arnold
Geo Boothroyd
Eugene A. Braman
August Buchaltz
Henry W. Cady
Reil Catlin
Alonzo W. Cobb
Geo W. Cook
Richard W. Devore
Alfred Eastman
Thos Fagan
John Hennings
John Henze
Edward A. Hodge
Arnold Hollman
Gustave Johnson
Elias F. Kimball
John A. Leeson
*Eli N. Lewis
*Wm. Luchan

Niles P. Malmborg
Joseph H. Miner
*Henry Morse
G. Nasland
John Nelson
Henry Nessen
Henry O' Kane
Ole O. Oskey
Wm. Perley
Aug Peterson
*Hans Peterson
John N. Pettibone
Joseph Pickering
Benj R. Prince
*Peter Schwetzscher
Ferd Shoemaker
Geo Simmons
Dwight Tillotson
Peter Tubbesing
Joshua A. Tupper
Nathan W. Tupper
David E. Todd
H. Van Anken
*Alonzo C. Wakefield
Chas H. Watson
John K. Wood

Company "G."

Organized August 1862 - From St. Paul
(Remained at Camp Atchison.)

Captain Charles J. Stees, Commissioned 2nd Lieut., August 12, 1862.
2nd Lieut. Henry H. Gilbert.
Captain Valentine, August 19; resigned.
1st Serg't Orlo Rogers, Appointed August 19, 1862.
2nd Serg't Horace N. Randall, January 16, 1863.
3rd Serg't James S. Connellee, October 12, 1862.
4th Serg't A. C. Helmkamp, October 12, 1862.
5th Serg't Isaac D. Morgan, January 16, 1863.
1st Corporal Frederick Iltis, August 19, 1862.
2nd Corporal Edwin L. Fryer, August 19, 1862.
3rd Corporal Edwin J. VanSlyke, August 19, 1862.
4th Corporal William Wallace, January 16, 1863.
5th Corporal Ed. O. Zimmermann, January 16, 1863.
6th Corporal G. P. Reynolds, January 16, 1863.
7th Corporal David Guerin, January 16, 1863.
8th Corporal L. W. Middlebrooks, January 16, 1863.

Musician
Franklin G. Brawley

Bugler
Henry F. Gross

Wagoner
Thomas J. Stokes

Privates

Wm. H. Abbott
Zeph Archambeau
Peter Barbeau
Geo M. Brack
John B. Carle
Dennis Cherrier
Alonzo Colman
Melvin L. Colman
Wm Eilers
L. Eisenmenger
Geo Germin
Ole Goodman
Jos Hare Jr.
G. S. Haseltine
W. L. Johnson
Ed H. Judson
H. F. J. Knieff
Ceril Labelle
Theophile Lefevre

◊Xavia Maunhart
H. D. Matthews
Hans D. McCloud
Geo Mead
Peter Molitor
John H. Myrick
Ed C. Palmer
M. H. Patterson
G. Prudhomme
John D. Rackliffe
Anton Rohl
J. M. Siebenthalen
John Staus
Franz Stoltz
John Sutheimer
Thos J. Stokes
Arch Thompson
John Way
Harvey N. Wilmot
Pomeroy Wilson
Chas A. Zimmermann

Company "H."

Organized August 18, 1862 - From Olmsted County.

Capt. Wm. K. Tattersall, Commissioned August 20, 1862.
1st Lieut. Samuel Geisinger, August 20.
2nd Lieut. William Brown, August 20.
1st Serg't Wm. M. Evans, Appointed August 20, 1862.
2nd Serg't Silas Avery, August 20, 1862.
3rd Serg't John Robinson, August 20, 1862.
4th Serg't Benjamin McDowell, January 1, 1863.
5th Serg't Libbeus White, March 10, 1863.
1st Corporal Franklin Sylvester, August 20, 1862.
2nd Corporal Wm. P. Burgan, August 20, 1862.
*3rd Corporal Aaron Hill, August 20, 1862.
4th Corporal Reuben Black, August 20, 1862.
5th Corporal Menzo Wood, January 1, 1863.
6th Corporal John H. King, January 1, 1863.
7th Corporal James C. Patton, March 10, 1863.
8th Corporal Amos Hyatt, March 10, 1863.

Wagoner
Mortimer H. Ireland

Privates

Morgan L. Bulen
Wm. Bursan
David C. Bentley
David W. Bradley
Robt C. Bitner
Americus Boright
Harry Brown
Chas W. Brooks
Wm R. Brooks
Jas A. Blair
*Geo Chilson
John T. Collins
Wm. H. Collins
Albert S. Chase
W. H. Chamberlain
Silas Cole
Dan H. Crego
John Caffers
Arthur M. Daniels
Callender Ditter
◊Herbert N. Everts
Alfred L. Fross
Marcus B. Felt
Otto Grodewohl
Robt Garrard
*Richard A. Hoag
Jerome Harrington

Jas J. Hume
Theron S. Higbe
*Chas J. Johnson
Wm Jones
Ed M. Kitchell
◊Wm D. Lovelace
Sidney Newell
Thos B. Olds
Harmon A. Page
John S. Page
John D. Parish
Charles N. Payne
Jerome P. Patten
Chas W. Russell
Lafayette Roat
Frank A. Remmick
George Risley
Robert Simonton
*Dan D. Smith
*W. J. Speed
E. B. Speed
Lucien Stewart
And Simmons
Randolph Seaman
*Ed A. Seaman
◊D. H. Tyler
*David Talmon
◊Geo H. Woodbury
Joseph N. Woods
Stephen O. Weston
John Yates

Company "I."

Organized August, 1862.

Captain Thomas I. Slaughter, Commissioned February 10, 1863;
    1st Lieut. August 20, 1862.
1st Lieut. Robert Hasty, February 10, 1863; 2nd Lieut. August 20, 1862.
2nd Lieut. Edward A. O'Brien, February 10, 1863; 1st Serg't August 20, 1862.
1st Serg't Wm. G. Gresham, Appointed March 1, 1863.
2nd Serg't Theodore E. Parker, March 1, 1863.
3rd Serg't Frank M. Thornton, March 1, 1863.
4th Serg't Samuel O'Brien, March 1, 1863.
5th Serg't John W. Peterson, March 1, 1863.
1st Corporal Peter A. Lungren, March 1, 1863.
2nd Corporal Melvin H. Bromley, March 1, 1863.
3rd Corporal W. Van Valkenberg, March 1, 1863.
4th Corporal James Y. Avery, March 1, 1863.
5th Corporal John W. Black, March 1, 1863.
6th Corporal Francis E. Daggett, March 1, 1863.
7th Corporal Gilman K. McKusick, March 1, 1863.
8th Corporal Ezra A. Cooper, March 1, 1863.

Privates

Florence J. Alden
Chas Anderson
Oliver F. Beale
Frank Benjamin
John Bennett
*John R. Barker
*Sam Bennett
H. M. L. J. Brown
◊John Carlson
J. A. Carpenter
Sam Clapshaw
Wm Clark
Jas H. Cornell
Geo R. Crippen
Anthony J. Crisp
John A. Darling
John Duffy
Fielding F. Enfield
John Farmer
Simeon Furber
Wm Frankland
Michael Heszler
Chester D. Hill
Thos Hoelson
*Jos January
*Lewis January

Notto Jenson
Orlando M. Kerr
Wm H. Lord
Thos Marshall
Nicholas Moren
*And Munson
John Nelson
J. A. Nelson
◊Wm H. Olliver
Hans P. Olsen
Olavius Olsen
John Peterson
Wm L. Pike
Wm H. Pryor
John L. Reed
Syver C. Rukki
Asa Scott
John Shalen
Wesley Shullenburger
Martin B. Smith
Ole S. Soren
Jonathan Summers
David O. Thing
Japie Trulson
Sam S. Waggoner
Douglas Whitney
John Williams

Company "K."

Organized August 17, 1862 - From Houston and Filmore Counties.

Captain William W. Braden, Commissioned January 5, 1863;
   1st Lieut. August 19, 1862.
2nd Lieut. Charles L. Gayle, January 5, 1863; enlisted as Wagoner.
2nd Serg't David C. Miller, February 7, 1863.
3rd Serg't Charles E. Massey, February 7, 1863.
4th Serg't Charles Chapman, February 7, 1863.
*5th Serg't John Gunn, February 7, 1863.
1st Corporal John C. Shelby, August 22, 1862.
2nd Corporal Carlos P. Gould, February 13, 1863.
3rd Corporal Henry Pennick, August 22, 1862.
4th Corporal Horatio Selfridge, February 13, 1863.
5th Corporal Alfred Drury, August 22, 1862.
*6th Corporal John H. Brown, February 13, 1863.
7th Corporal Alfred Haskins, August 22, 1862.
8th Corporal James Franklin, August 22, 1862.

Musicians

Edwin Morey   Leland P. Smith

Privates

◊Wm Andrews
Jacob Apple
Peter Berger
Ole O. Bursom
Luther Burrows
*Jas Carlin
Robt Crowell
*L. D. Churchill
Joseph Curry
M. W. Dennison
◊Alex I. Douchey
Robt Douglas
Patrick Dugan
John Fair
Nicholas Fish
Oramel Gould
Geo Guivits
Jacob Heshler
Halver Halverson
Ed A. Keeler
Philip Ketzinger
Abraham Lang
Lionel C. Long
J. C. Loutzenheizer
Michael Mander
John Matthias

Jas McDonald
  wagoner
M. McDonald
Joseph McPherson
Theodore D. Miller
*Martin Miller
F. Miller
James Neal
Albert Newberry
Jas Newberry
John S. Offey
*Jas Ostrander
Ross Phillips
Matthias Rooster
H. H. Selfridge
R. R. Scisson
Oliver P. Sprague
Geo W. Srouf
Wm J. Stewart
Geo Thomas
John Wellington
*John Whitlow
Ezra O. Wisel
Alvah Wright

Seventh Regiment, M. V.
Field and Staff

Lieut. Colonel William R. Marshall, August 28; private August 13, 1862.
Major George Bradley, September 5; 2nd Lieut. August 13, 1862.
Adjutant Edward A. Trader, May 30, 1863; Serg't Major September 5, 1862.
Quartermaster Ammi Cutter, August 22; private August 13, 1862.
Surgeon Lucius B. Smith, May 29, 1863; 1st Assistant October 30, 1862.
2nd Assistant do Albert A. Ames, August 28; private August 14, 1862.
Sergeant Major Andrew J. Patch, Appointed June 18, 1863; private Co. F.
Com. Sergeant Christopher C. Griderian, October 1, 1862; private,
    transferred from 10th Regiment.
Q. M. Sergeant Edward H. Wood, December 23, 1862; private Co. C.
Hospital Steward Richard E. Traver, September 1, 1862; private Co. F.
Principal Musician Erastus Guard, May 1, 1863.
Wagon Master Charles Bingham, from Co. A

Company "A."

Organized August 1862 - From Rice County.

Captain John K. Arnold, Commissioned May 29, 1863.
1st Lieut. Loren B. Hoag, August 16, 1862.
2nd Lieut. Wm. W. Willis, June 19, 1863.
*2nd Lieut. C. Barrack, resigned.
1st Sergeant Daniel Goodhue, Appointed July 1, 1863.
2nd Serg't L. E. Hanneman, August 19, 1862.
3rd Serg't Charles P. Anderson, August 19, 1862.
*4th Serg't Richard C. Ross, October 12, 1862.
5th Serg't Samuel S. Averill, July 1, 1863.
1st Corporal Geo. L. Kendall, August 19, 1862.
2nd Corporal Edwin Gillett, August 19, 1862.
3rd Corporal Daniel O. Searles, August 19, 1862.
4th Corporal Lyman B. Snow, August 19, 1862.
5th Corporal Doran F. Kelly, August 19, 1862.
*6th Corporal Henry Marsh, August 19, 1862.
7th Corporal John A. Bond, July 1, 1863.
8th Corporal George Deck, July 1, 1863.

Musicians
*Michael Anderson   *Alex A. Bates.

Wagoner   **Bugler**
Henry Finley   Oscar J. Webster

Privates

Myron M. Austin	John More
Henry Barrett	Ed McKenzie
John Beardslee	Joseph Miner
Amos Bice	Wm H. McDonald
Lemuel Cone	◊Wm Marshall
A. A. Caulkins	Dan A. Parke
Elijah Carpenter	M. C. Peasley
Peter DeLancey	*Peter Ramsdell
Philo F. Englesby	*Wm D. Rounce
Jos Fredenburg	Philip Rich
Albert Fredenburg	And Robinson
Michael Fitzgerrold	Erick Rinde
Dan Goodsell	Wm K. Ross
*Wm T. Gassner	Wm W. Sidwell
Frank Goen	*Amaziah Slocum
Chas Holt	*Adam Smith
*John R. Horner	Wm L. Stevens
Issac Johnson	Peter Simon
Frank Kendall	John W. Thompson
M. Lockwood	Alvin B. Thorp
John Mullen	*Albert Tripp
Peter Morgan	Chas Vicant
Homer P. More	Roland Veeks
	*Geo Wells

Company "B."

Organized August 11, 1862 - From Winona County.

Captain Albert H. Stevens, Commissioned June 4, 1862.
2nd Lieut. Ermond D. Eastman, June 4, 1862.
1st Serg't John W. Wilson, Appointed June 16, 1863.
2nd Serg't James McDonald, August 17, 1862.
3rd Serg't Robert F. Norton, March 1, 1863.
4th Serg't George E. Morrill, May 23, 1863.
5th Serg't Myron Toms, June 16, 1863.
1st Corporal Henry G. Bilbie, August 17, 1862.
2nd Corporal Stephen Mills, August 17, 1862.
3rd Corporal Sam'l H. Harrison, August 17, 1862.
4th Corporal James T. Ramer, August 17, 1862.
5th Corporal Edwin C. Hinkley, October 11, 1862.
6th Corporal Joseph Lamay, January 14, 1863.
7th Corporal Alva E. Dearborn, May 23, 1863.
8th Corporal Alfred Bartlett, June 16, 1863.

Musician	**Bugler**
John Pritchard	Frank C. Richardson

Privates

Ethan Allen
Geo Blackwell
Chas Billings
*Henry Balcom,
    Brigade P M
Wm Burns
Geo W. Buswell
Geo L. Colburn
Nap Chamberlain
Collins Covey
*John Clears
*Harry Clark
*Robert Cully
Edward Dowling
Daniel Dana
David Dribblebliss
Benj F. Every
Maurice J. Fletcher
John Hughes
Thos Hanley
Brazilla B. Howe
Joseph Hazen
Jas R. Howell
John R. Harris

Albert J. Hough
Watson I. Lampson
James Monk
Jeremiah Murphy
John W. Moore
Winburn F. Marsh
*Noah D. Marsh
Isaac M. May
Edwin S. Metcalf
Geo P. Nicholas
John B. Preswick
*Douglas J. Pierson
Philetus A. Philipps
Wm P. Rodgers
Ernst Shuman
Leander Slade
Morris W. Taylor
Urich Toman
Jeptha Turner
*Alanson Turner
*Sam G. Wright
*Aurelius Wilgus
Levi Ward

Company "C."

Organized August 16, 1862 - From Washington and Chisago Counties.

Captain William H. Burt, Commissioned August 21, 1862.
1st Lieut. Frank H. Pratt, May 26, 1863.
2nd Lieut.Wm. H. Thomas, May 26, 1863.
1st Serg't H. F. Folsom, Appointed July 1, 1863.
3rd Serg't Ephraim H. Pray, August 24, 1862.
4th Serg't Howard F. Oliver, August 24, 1862.
5th Serg't Jerry T. Jillison, August 24, 1862.
1st Corporal Andrew Agren, July 1,1863.
2nd Corporal Peter Anderson, August 24, 1862.
*3rd Serg't John S. Johnson, August 24, 1862.
4th Serg't Oran Richardson, August 24 1862.
5th Serg't Wm. Carnithan, August 24, 1862.
6th Serg't Vacant
7th Serg't Joseph Clendening, August 24, 1862.
 8th Serg't Andrew C. Colby, August 24, 1862.

Privates

And P. Anderson
Swen Anderson
Carl Anderson
John Ayers
Jared W. Bellaney
John Bloom
John P. Baik
John C. Carlson
Nulan M. Chase
*James Coop
⚑John Carpenter
*Sam S. Colby
John Carlson
Frank Carlson
Thos Crisswell
Peter Charlson
Peter J. Carlson
And Dahlstrom
*Wm S. Dedon
*Henry F. Day
*John Elmquist
Dan Fredin
⚑Wyman X. Folsom
Carl Glader
⚑Jas M. Gitchell
Alex Givens
Wm H. Gray
Dennis Huntley
Edw Herrick
Ole H. Holmber
Joel A. Hickerson
Perry D. Hickerson
Carl Johnson
Peter Johnson
John Kelsey

Hiram Lawton
John Lonquist
Geo B. Lea
Magnus Monson
Chas Martin
Israel Magnuson
Thos F. Morton
Nils Nilson
John Nilson
Dan Nelson
Swen Nelson
Wm H. Norway
John Olson
Hendrick Ostrand
Henry F. Otis
◊Simon E. Persons
Albert Pehrson
Gust Petterson
Magnus Peterson
John Palm
*Nels Rosengreen
Geo W. Simons
*Lucius W. Snell
Carl Sakison
⚑Herbert H. Stone
*Olaf A. Strom
⚑Peter A. Strand
And Smith
John S. Swenson
Af Sherquist
Hiram M. Thomas
Francis Thomas
Fred Tang
Stephen E. Tollman

Company "C." stayed at Camp Atchison, and went to Devils Lake.

Company "D."

Organized August 20, 1862 - From Winona County.

Captain Rolla Banks, Commissioned August 22, 1862.
1st Lieut. Norman Buck, August 22, 1862.
2nd Lieut. Zebediah W. Marsh, August 22, 1862.
1st Serg't Mart Robinson, Appointed August 18, 1862.
*2nd Serg't Malcolm Clark, August 18, 1862.

3rd Serg't Franklin Videto, August 18, 1862.
4th Serg't James M. Canfield, August 18, 1862.
5th Serg't Chas D. Kenyon, August 24, 1862.
1st Corporal Matt. H. Monahon, August 24, 1862.
2nd Corporal Helkiah Lilly, August 24, 1862.
3rd Corporal Frank M. Webb, August 24, 1862.
4th Corporal Louis P. Grant, August 24, 1862.
5th Corporal Geo. A. Carsley, August 24, 1862.
6th Corporal Thos. Davidson, August 24, 1862.
7th Corporal Levi B. Whitlock, August 24, 1862.
8th Corporal Fletcher C. Harvey, April 1863.

Musicians

*Wm. Shay   *Oliver P. Gates

Wagoner   **Bugler**
John Morrison   Jefferson Bathrick

Privates

Isaac C. Bertrand	John Hanley
Chas Brewer	John K. Howe
Chas L. Blair	Melzer Hutton
Albert C. Buck	*Edw D. Jackson
*John Bolin	*Horace E. Jeffrey
John Bissett	Jos P. Kendricks
John B. Berry	*Levi D. Libby
Jas P. Berry	Benson Lee
Alson Barton	Gardner W. Lee
Edwin Brown	*Dan G. Leighton
Chas L. Berghart	Wm Montgomery
Dudley C. Cass	Malcom C. Mott
Dan M. Cooper	Sam McCann
Gilbert Corey	Arnold Newcomb
Dan H. Cheney	Stephen L. Northru
John Cripps	Wm O'Hara
Albert J. Clark	Edgar A. Perkins
A. B. Clark	Geo W. Richardson
Robt W. Davidson	*Dan Steadman
Jas Davis	Benj F. Schafner
John A. Dickson	Wm Small
Geo H. Elsbury	M J Thomas
Eugene Fay	Mark Thompson
Jud W. Fuller	Calvin J. Vance
A. H. Fuller	Jacob Van Slyke
Geo M. French	Edw D. Wilmot
Arnold W. Grout	*Chas F. Wegener
Oren Grout	And Wingent
*Edw D. Gilbert	
H. C. Hitchcock	
H. W. Hughes	
Irvine M. Hill	

Company "D." went to Fort Abercrombie, September 23, 1862; remained till July 6, 1863, and then joined Regiment at Camp Hayes and went with Expedition.

Company "E."

Organized August 15, 1862 - From Fillmore County.

Captain Thomas G. Hall, Commissioned September 25, 1862.
1st Lieut. Lewis Hardy, June 11, 1863; promoted from 2nd Lieut.
1st Serg't J. C. McCormick, Appointed November 1, 1862.
*2nd Lieut. John M. Neely, November 1, 1862.
3rd Lieut. Ferd A. Elder, November 1, 1862.
4th Lieut. John M'Gown, November 1, 1862.
5th Lieut. Maxson L. Potter, November 1, 1862.
1st Corporal George W. Graham, November 1, 1862.
*2nd Corporal Calvin Hoag, November 1, 1862.
3rd Corporal Ransom Walter, November 1, 1862.
*4th Corporal T. D. Broughton, November 1, 1862.
*5th Corporal Edwin Stork, November 1, 1862.
6th Corporal Ara Plomteaux, November 1, 1862.
7th Corporal Arne Arneson, November 1, 1862.
8th Corporal Martin Henderson, November 1, 1862.

Privates

Ole O. Bagley
M. J. Butler
Beriah Bliss
Milton Burous
Gerry S. Burdick
John Blackburn
Michael Bennett
Chris Christopherson
Geo W. Craig
Omar H. Case
Jos Daniels
Barnabas Dawson
J. T. Drummond
W. E. Drummond
W. E. Durand
*A. H. H. Dayton
Notley D. Elless
L. D. Emmons
James H. Fitch
Geo S. Farquer
Lucien B. Finch
Jacob B. Gaage
*Peter Gibney
Chas Gorton
Freeman E. Guptil
Dan Hill
Mike T. Hagland
Rasmus Hausker
*Angel Hausker
*Alfred Hull
*Jeremiah Huyck

W. S. Ingals
John W. Jones
Lars Johnson
John Jacobson
Albert Lloyd
J. C. Larson
Jas M'Gown
Ira Morey
Olans Oleson
*Peter Peterson
*Chas H. Perry
*David A. Pierce
Ed H. Rensberger
Wesley Stevens
Chas Schultz
*Philander Sayles
Emory D. Seelye
Frank M. Stebbins
Theodore Tousley
Thos Thompson
Thos P. Thompson
Chas S. Warr
Geo L. Walker
Spencer J. Wilbur

Company "F."

Organized August 19, 1862 - From Dakota County.

Captain John Kennedy, Commissioned August 25, 1862.
1st Lieut. Lorenzo W. Collins, January 2, 1863; promoted from 2nd Lieut.
2nd Lieut. Stephen C. Miller, January 2, 1863; transferred from 6th Regiment.
1st Serg't Stephen H. Dickens, Appointed August 26, 1862.
2nd Serg't Alonzo H. Wood, August 26, 1862.
3rd Serg't John G. Martz, August 26, 1862.
4th Serg't John A. Moulton, August 26, 1862.
5th Serg't John More, August 26, 1862.
1st Corporal John L. Hoover, August 26, 1862.
2nd Corporal Geo. A. Wheeler, August 26, 1862.
5th Corporal Chas H. Atkinson, August 26, 1862.
6th Corporal Albert W. Newell, November 20, 1862.
*7th Corporal Joel M. Darling, December 30, 1862.
8th Corporal W. H. Jarvis, jr., March 25, 1863.

Musician
Arthur Fish

Bugler
Henry Nivarel

Wagoner
Elias Ballard

Privates

Eli Ballard
Hiram Burgess
Hugh Bradley
◊R. Brawand
Jos W. Bottomly
Jacob Buckman
Jed Bennett
Orson Corson
Oct P. Chamberlain
Mart H. Countryman
Edw Dungay
*Alonzo E. Day
Fred J. Dean
Hugh Duffy
Jacob Dunlinger
Sam Ells
Nicholas Eischen
Chas Fisher
*Amasa A. Farmer
*Anson G. Foster
Anthony Faecker
Francis W. Geiger
Peter Gergen
Robt Gregg
And J. Heaguy
And M. Hunt
Michael Haas

Jas H. Holmes
Wm Henderson
Caleb Hosford
Elias W. Holden
John Irthum
*Jas A. Jeffers
N. C. Johnson
Chas Johnson
Wm Johnson
Nicholas Kassel
Owen Kennard
John A. Morton
Edw L. Moizo
Archer Masters
*John Merwin
Jas McDowell
Israel C. Morey
John Mahoney
*Dan Purcell
*Ira Putman
Jos A. Smith
H. D. Smith
Fred A. Stier
Stephen Schmall
Obediah V. Veley
*H. O. Vaninwagen
Thos Wilson
Zimri Harrison

Company "G."

Organized August 17, 1862 - From Goodhue County.

Captain Wm. C. Williston, Commissioned August 26, 1862.
1st Lieut. Herman Betcher, August 20, 1862.
2nd Lieut. Daniel Densmore, August 20, 1862.
1st Serg't James A. Owens, August 28, 1862.
*2nd Serg't Manville Comstock, August 28, 1862.
3rd Serg't Wm. M. Philles, August 28, 1862.
4th Serg't Abe L. Jackson, August 28, 1862.
*5th Serg't Jacob Christ, August 28, 1862.
1st Corporal John W. Jefferson, August 28, 1862.
*2nd Corporal Fred Remshardt, August 28, 1862.
3rd Corporal Ole T. Berg, August 28, 1862.
4th Corporal Hiram Cadwell, November 21, 1862.
5th Corporal Jacob L. Hamlin, April 4, 1863.
6th Corporal Patrick Fury, May 1, 1863.
*7th Corporal Ole E. Strand, August 28, 1862.
8th Corporal Henry P. McIntyre, August 28, 1862.

Musician
Wm. R. Wray

Bugler
Ole A. Strand

Privates

Michael Ackaman
Arne Anderson
And Anderson
Harry Britell
Ben Benson
Sam Budd
Nelson Bergh
Truman E. Beers
*Freeman T. Beers
Henry K. Carson
Jacob Cook Jr
Stephen G. Cady
Timothy Cavanaugh
Hans H. Danielson
John Danielson
Peter Engberg
*Fred Ehlert
Mart Edwards
Timothy Foley
Peter E. Fladland
Fort Hempling
Herman Hempling
Aug G. Hillig
Isaac P. Hilton
Clark V. Hubbard
Englebert Hollie
Hans Havelson

John F. Hutchison
John Johnson
John A. Johnson
Peter Johnson
Toller Johnson
Wm King
Kaspar Koch
Orrin C. Leonard
John Manson
Francis McMahan
*N. J. Mageras
John Manion
*John Olson Jr
John A. Olson
Ole Olson
*Eric Olson
*John F. Peterson
Robt Percival
Sidney W. Park
Jonas Swan
Chas J. Sundell
*Russell E. Snell
Jacob Schneider
Fred Thiergen
Peter Wagner Jr

Company "H."

Organized September 1, 1862 - From Sibley and Ramsey Counties.

Captain James Gilfillan, Commissioned September 1, 1862.
1st Lieut. S. Lee Davis, February 13, 1863; 2nd Lieut. September 1, 1862.
2nd Lieut. Chauncey B. Wilkinson, April 23, 1863;
   5th Serg't September 1, 1862.
*1st Serg't Simeon P. Folsom, Appointed January 16, 1863.
2nd Serg't Davis Newell, September 15, 1862.
3rd Serg't Charles Bonarth, December 1, 1862.
4th Serg't Thomas Scantleburg, February 3, 1863.
5th Serg't Wm. Maurer, March 1, 1863.
1st Corporal Andrew Witte, September 15, 1862.
2nd Serg't Henry L. Mills, September 15, 1862.
3rd Serg't Chas. Wackerhagen, September 15, 1862.
4th Serg't Edward F. Wright, September 15, 1862.
*5th Serg't Hans Hansen, September 15, 1862.
6th Serg't George Asal, March 1, 1863.
*7th Serg't Wm. Whitehill, March 1, 1863.
8th Serg't E. S. Lightbourne, April 26, 1863.

Musicians

*Lester B. Winslow   Jeremiah J. Cantwell

Wagoner

John Gibe

Privates

Michael Bellair	Orson C. Murray
John Bloom	Joseph Nigg
Sam Borth	Anton Peltz
John Brennan	Henry Pohl
Conrad Buesing	*John Polzin
*Edw Camarind	Harmon Reimer
John Cheney	John L. Ruth
Ira Cole	Henry Schaeffer
*Fred H. Fessenden	H. L. Schaeffer
John Gerken	Edw Schuetz
Seffrin Gondreau	Aug Steiehm
John Griggs	Wm Stringer
Franz Grassinger	*Chris Surber
Chas T. Groot	Bernard H. Theders
Anthony Gress	Chris N. Troxel
*H. J. Hagadorn	Geo Troxel
Jacob Harisburger	W. H. Troxel
Stephen Jarvis	John G. Veeh
Fred Jarvis	And P. Walker
*Fred Junge	Robt B. Wade
Ed Klappenbach	Fred Wagge
Albert Koblinger	Conrad Warnecke
*Bernard Krieger	*Ludwig Weckwerth
Louis Leferier	John Winter
Gordon Legg	Chas Woehler
Nap L'Heureux	*J. Wollendorf
Henry Luss	
*Joseph Krnshe	
Jas C. Mullin	

Company "I."

(Remained at Camp Atchison.)

Organized August 23, 1862 - From Stearns, Morrison and Benton Counties.

Captain Asa Libby, Jr., Commissioned September 2, 1862.
1st Lieut. James M. McKelvy, September 2, 1862.
2nd Lieut. George Mayhew, August 12, 1862.
1st Serg't P. W. Laughlin, Appointed August 25, 1862.
2nd Serg't Josiah E. West, September 6, 1862.
3rd Serg't James K. Miller, September 6, 1862.
4th Serg't Samuel C. Johnson, September 6, 1862.
5th Serg't D. McDougall, March 2, 1863.
1st Corporal Allen E. Hussey, September 6, 1862.
2nd Corporal Hiram Sanders, September 6, 1862.
3rd Corporal Wm. Darnell, September 6, 1862.
4th Corporal Ephraim Curtis, September 6, 1862.
5th Corporal Chas. R. Sylvester, September 6, 1862.
6th Corporal Harry Sawyer, September 6, 1862.
◊7th Corporal Jonas D. Thomas, March 2, 1863.
8th Corporal Van R. Getchell, March 2, 1863.

Musician
◊Lawrence Garlington

Wagoner
Timothy Hurley

Privates

Joseph Adams
Uriah F. Allen
Nathan Bates
Abe D. Brower
Robt Biggerstaff
John Bowen
◊Sam A. Blood
Simon D. Barnes
Michael P. Beckley
Chas F. Bowhall
And M. Chapman
Geo S. Christler
Geo Chamberlain
Geo Crow
Isaac Carter
John Dressler
John B. Dearing
Dan B. Fisk
Jos H. Fadden
Chas A. Fadden
Abe French
Levi S. Geer
Nathaniel Grant
Geo Glover
Clifton B. Gregory
A. B. Hogdon
Chris Hart
Edw Hart

David Harvey
J. D. Hoffman
Geo Jones
Byron Lent
◊Flaven Lemay
Henry Myers
H. W. A. Mergel
Dan Martin
Amos McGee
Dan McArthur
Jonathan L. Nash
John Owens
John C. Pinckney
Wm Rocicot
Benj R. Rackliff
Alvah K. Ridley
Alonzo Smith
Joseph Stewart
Jas Sullivan
Jas Summers
Nathaniel R. Spurr
John Vezey
Chas T. Wood
Chris Wilkins
Gouvin W. Wilson

Company "K."

Organized August 19, 1862 - From LeSueur County.
Captain Theodore G. Carter, Commissioned February 24, 1863; promoted from 1st Lieut.
1st Lieut. Felix A. Bouer, February 24, 1863; promoted from 2nd Lieut.
2nd Lieut. Nelson H. Manning, February 24; promoted from 1st Serg't.
1st Serg't James B. Turrittin, Appointed March 9, 1863.
2nd Serg't Dan E. Williams, August 19, 1862.
*3rd Serg't Wm. J. Worden, August 19, 1862.
4th Serg't Wm. Lancaster, August 19, 1862.
*5th Serg't Nathan L. Carter, March 9, 1863.
1st Corporal George C. Clapp, August 19, 1862.
2nd Corporal Frank A. Wildes, August 19, 1862.
3rd Corporal John S. Turrittin, August 19, 1862.
4th Corporal Benj. R. Damrin, August 19, 1862.
5th Corporal Thos. Montgomery, August 19, 1862.
7th Corporal Archibald Savidge, November 21, 1862.
8th Corporal Edward L. Johnson, March 9, 1863.

Musician
Morgan Kingsley

Wagoner
Lawson Hill

Bugler
Joseph Schepperle

Privates

John Arend
*Philander Brown
Herman Borer
Seth Birdsall
*Timothy M. Connor
John W. Chambers
*Jas H. Cooley
*Chas O. Chapman
Sam H. Connor
*D. A. Canfield
Michael Dorn
Timothy B. Davis
Joseph Davis
John Diller
W. W. Douglass
John Dahlmann
Thos Fitch
Henry Fruchte
Manley Grover
Thos Haley
*Thos B. Hobson
Robt Holcomb
Marion Harrier
John N. Hess
Chas E. Hess
Thos Hannigan
*Jas N. Hoyt
Homer F. Hallock

Patrick Hoey
Jos Hermann
Anton Huck
David Johnson
C. C. Kendall
Michael Keogh
Wm Lauer
*Cyrus P. Little
Jas McNeil
Paddock Morris
*Peter McCabe
Thos E. Nason
Herman Ostwald
Chas C. Pettis
Emanuel Reyff
Eusebius Reyff
Henry S. Sigley
Geo Simpson
Ed R. R. Talbot
Oliver C. Tibbets
*Edw Tolan
°Mart Weissenriether
*And Wilfret
Jas F. Westlake

° Sent back to Mankato from Camp Hayes.

Tenth Regiment
Field and Staff

Colonel James H. Baker, Commissioned November 17, 1862.
Lieut. Colonel Samuel P. Jennison, September 10, 1862.
Major Michael Cook, September 15, 1862; Adjutant 2nd Minnesota Volunteers.
Quartermaster George W. Green, October 8, 1862.
Surgeon Samuel B. Sheardown, October 16, 1862.
1st Assistant Wm. W. Clark, September 10, 1862.
2nd do Alfred M. Burham, October 11, 1862.
Chaplain Ezra R. Lathrop
Sergeant Major A. C. Flander, December 2, 1862.
Q. M. Sergeant Richard Siewer, December 15, 1862; from Company B.
Com. Sergeant Lorin S. Meeker, December 2, 1862; from Company K.
Hospital Steward Louis Probesting, October 23, 1862; from Company E.
Principal Musician George A. Todd, from Company E.

Company "A."

Organized August 17, 1862.

Captain Rufus C. Ambler, Commissioned August 18, 1862.
1st Lieut. Lewis F. Babcock, August 18, 1862.
2nd Lieut. M. L. Strong, August 18, 1862.
1st Sergeant Smith A. Stowers, Appointed September 8, 1862.
2nd Serg't Andrew J. Rideout, August 8, 1862.
3rd Serg't Hubbard N. Thurston, August 8, 1862.
4th Serg't Willard E. Martin, August 8, 1862.
5th Serg't Arza B. Thompson, August 8, 1862.
1st Corporal Eben M. Guile, August 8, 1862.
2nd Corporal John L. Barney, August 8, 1862.
3rd Corporal John H. Bartley, August 8, 1862.
4th Corporal Frank A. Thompson, August 8, 1862.
5th Corporal Eugene P. King, August 8, 1862.
*6th Corporal Joseph R. Webster, August 8, 1862.
*7th Corporal Benj. C. Sanborn, August 8, 1862.
8th Corporal Hugh Burns, August 8, 1862.

Privates

James H. Adams
Levi Annis
Warren P. Bissell
Hugh Burns
Wm Barnhard
Jas Barnhard
Jacob S. Bixby
Jacob Berg
*Jud J. Barnes
Ferd Borchert
Calvin G. Bliss
Thos J. Curtis
Sam J. Curtis
Chas C. Curtis
*Geo W. Curtis
Dexter Carlton
Joseph Carpenter
Frank Chambers
Henry Deopfing
Thos E. Davis
◊Richard M. Drake
A. R. Eastman
Geo W. Euny
*Levi Flake
Lorain Fowler
*Sam M. Freeman
*John Farrell
*Wm Green
Asa S. Haynes
*Wm Harty
Jacob W. Hess
*Chas Hammon
◊John A. Heath
Sanford E. Hayes

Chas Jeffry
John McCrora
Henry B. Jones
*A. W. Jones
Geo Kendig
Stillman Kinney
John Lane
Albert McKinney
*Frank Melvin
Orland S. Moore
*Jas Naylor
John B. Norman
Geo C. Pettie
*Cyrenius B. Pettie
*Elias G. Pike
Chas Pomeroy
And W. Reed
◊Isaac Reese
Wm H. Russell
Jonathan Show
Emmons P. Taylor
Dem L. Winchell
*Melvin H. Welch
John M. Warfield
Walter M. Wheeler
John Morris
W. W. Williams
*Henry Pasce
Wm Pasce
*Wm Scott
Isaac Vail
*Zeno S. Yearley

Company "B."

Organized August 14, 1862 - From Dodge County.

Captain Alonzo J. Edgerton, Commissioned August 21, 1861.
1st Lieut. Wm. McMicken, August 19, 1862.
2nd Lieut. Samuel Burwell, August 15, 1862.
1st Serg't Thos J. Hunt, Appointed August 22, 1862.
2nd Serg't Charles D. Tuthill, August 22, 1862.
3rd Serg't Alonzo G. Edgerton, August 22, 1862.
4th Serg't Clark Gleason, August 22, 1862.

5th Serg't Robert Moffit, August 22, 1862.
1st Corporal Geo. H. Newman, August 22, 1862.
2nd Corporal Charles J. Brace, August 22, 1862.
3rd Corporal F. W. Fellows, August 22, 1862.
4th Corporal John G. Merical, August 22, 1862.
5th Corporal Jesse Nunn, August 22, 1862.
6th Corporal Chris H. Fleaner, August 22, 1862.
*7th Corporal Amasa T. Miner.
8th Corporal James W. Beymer.

Musicians

*Willis D. L. Palmer   *Maurice H. Stevens

Bugler   **Wagoner**
Peter Young, Jr.   James N. Kinney

Privates

Freeman Andrews
Peter Anderson
Wm Baumann
*Leander F. Baxter
Wm M. Bosley
Chas H. Brown
S J. Bosworth
*Edgar Bentley
Alex Campbell
Geo Carlough
Peter Clark
Sam R. Cowen
Jas Cutsinger
John A. Cansdell
Chas N. Dailey
Freeman Durrell
Albert Farnsworth
Geo W. Fay
Benj Fuller
Henry Fleenar
Fred L. Garrison
Sam A. Gere
John Grems
*Christopher Gulson
Phlegmon Harter
*Jas Haman
*Jas R. Keith
Henry Keller
Isaac Keller
John V. Kendall
Durand Kimball
*Gilgen Klopenstein

*Hans Larson
*Jacob Larson
Ole Larson
Albert Lawrence
Homer B. Leavitt
Geo W. Mason
John Mastenbrook
Wm Mercer
Erastus F. Mallenger
Jacob Michael
Augustus C. Miller
H. M. Montgomery
Cornelius Moran
Felix Myers
Albert McIntyre
Wm J. McIntyre
Alfred Nichols
Wm H. Osborne
Thos D. Prentice
Richard W. Pierce
Homer E. Prindle
John Ratledge
Jos E. Rawlins
Wm Rice
E. B. Richardson
Dan W. Sherman Jr
A. W. Sherwood
Jas Stewart
Fred O. Stevens
Lafayette F Thompson
Thos H. Thompson
*Chas Van Allen
Nathan W. Waldo
Friend W. Wedman
*Stephen L. Wilson
Sanvin E. Woodward
Chas D. Younglove

Company "C."

Organized August 15, 1862 - From Wabashaw County.

Captain Charles W. Hackett, Commissioned August 23, 1862.
1st Lieut. Albert S. Hobson, August 23, 1862.
2nd Lieut. John Lathrop, August 23, 1862.
1st Serg't Wallace W. Case, Appointed September 2, 1862.
2nd Serg't Oliver K. Holcombe, September 2, 1862.
3rd Serg't John B. Robinson, September 2, 1862.
4th Serg't John W. Burnham, October 8, 1862.
2nd Corporal Francis W. Knapp, September 2, 1862.
3rd Corporal Arthur F. McKay, October 30, 1862.
4th Corporal Charles G. Dawley, September 2, 1862.
5th Corporal Henry Hipple, September 2, 1862.
6th Corporal Austin D. Carrell, September 2, 1862.
7th Corporal Francis H. Wilds, January 4, 1863.
8th Corporal James W. Hayes, June 1, 1863.

Musicians
Octavius A. Leland Thomas J. Cross

Wagoner
David Ackley

Privates

John M. Benthall
John Burton
Silas K. Burpee
*Clarence L. Buck
Frank M. Buck
Wm Canfield
Jas M. Collier
Thos Clipperton
Elanson H. Case
David E. Cross
Geo W. Drew
Almon H. Doeg
Peter Erickson
*Zelotes Foster
*Jas G. Foster
*Chas D. Foster
Gilbert F. Hancock
Hans Juelson
Geo W. Knowlton
Albert Linstrum
*Jas W. Lockey
Robt Moody
Eusebius Mullens
Edw H. Matterson
John W. Murphy

Geo A. Nicholson
*Dennis Nicholson
◊John Nelson
Chrest Nelson
*R. W. Olmsted
Collins Pratt
Jas R. Pope
Wm M. Pervis
Geo C. Putnam
Josiah A. Peck
Robt S. Rolph
Wm O. Sleeper
Henry Southwick
Christian Shilson
Henry Stuart
John L. Safford
Ebenezer L. Starr
Jas K. Tuft
*John D. Winter
Ogden D. Warner
*Horace B. Whiting
Dan Winter
Solomon Young
Dan Young
*Nathaniel Youman

Company "D."

Went to Devils Lake.

Captain Wm. W. Phelps, Commissioned September 8, 1862.
1st Lieut. Charles L. Davis, August 27, 1862.
2nd Lieut. Wm. B. Williams, September 8, 1862.
1st Serg't Henry A. McConnell, Appointed September 9, 1862.
2nd Serg't Theron B. McCord, September 9, 1862.
3rd Serg't Wm. A. Thompson, September 9, 1862.
4th Serg't Sam Kneitson, September 9, 1862.
5th Serg't John Winter, September 9, 1862.
1st Corporal Daniel Wightman, September 9, 1862.
2nd Corporal Francis D. Hill, September 9, 1862.
3rd Corporal Peter J. Johhson, September 9, 1862.
4th Corporal Henry H. Brown, September 9, 1862.
6th Corporal Thorston Opdahl, November 25, 1862.
7th Corporal Joseph Tapper, December 26, 1862.
8th Corporal Lewis Lewiston, July 19, 1863.

Wagoner
Ira E. Eggleston

Privates

Morgan Abel
Edward Amruan
Bour Anfindson
Henry Aspen
John Banks
Walter S. Barnes
Ulrick K. Berg
Serer Christopherson
Henry Erickson
Ole Evenson
Chas Falls
Oscar H. Freeman
Owen Gallagher
Jas R. Hart
Isaac G. Hasbrouck
Lemuel Herbert
Ole O. Hus
Chas C. Horton
Geo Johnson
Gunder Kellac
Bottal Larson
Ole Larson
Yares Larson
John K. Lyseng
John H. Miller
Leonard B. Mooers
Chas Nelson
Ole Nelson
John Nickels
Chas B. Noble
Edwin Olson
Mons Olson
Olans Olson
John Peterson
Geo Reeves
C. K. Ryalan
Nathan Satterley
Cyrus K. Smith
Halver Sondresom
Martin Stanhy
Torkel Svendson
Ingral Thoreson
David Wallower
Peter Wallower
Leander H. Watson
Chas M. Yates

Company "E."

Organized August 13, 1862 - From Freeborn County.

Captain John W. Heath, Commissioned November 11, 1862.
1st Lieut. Charles Kittlson, November 11, 1862.
2nd Lieut. Eli Ash, November 11, 1862.
*1st Serg't Eli K. Pickett, Appointed November 11, 1862.
2nd Serg't Geo. H. Partridge, November 11, 1862.
3rd Serg't Wm. H. Low, November 11, 1862.
4th Serg't James L. Cook, November 11, 1862.
5th Serg't George Osborne, November 11, 1862.
*1st Corporal John G. Dunning, November 11, 1862.
2nd Corporal H. D. Burlingame, November 11, 1862.
3rd Corporal J. W. Devereaux, November 11, 1862.
4th Corporal Rufus Kelley, November 11, 1862.
5th Corporal Alvah Stearns, November 11, 1862.
6th Corporal Christian Alspaugh, November 11, 1862.
7th Corporal Lars Wicks, November 11, 1862.
8th Corporal Daniel Anderson, November 11, 1862.

Musician
John L. Reynolds

Bugler
Leander J. Thomas

Wagoner
Asa Hard

Privates

Andrew Anderson
Stengrin Benson
Cyrus E. Bullock
*Lemuel E. Bullock
Henry C. Bartlett
Jas Boen
Andrew Black
Rodney M. Campbell
W. G. Carpenter
Daniel E. Consin
Fred O. Chamberlain
Francis Christianson
Francis M. Davis
*John Edson
Ingbert Errickson
*Geo Gates
Augustus Grobey
Godfrey Huber
◊L. D. Goldsbery
John Hoover
Ole Iverson
*Thos Iverson
Henry Johnson
*Eric C. Johnson

Uriah Judd
John C. Kaiser
Jas Lair
Patrick Morin
*Fred Maixner
Elijah M. Owen
Peter Olson
Israel H. Pace
Joel Past
*Isaac Perry
Benj Park
Cyrus Prescott
Chas Peterson
John Peterson
Robert Reynolds
Hiram J. Rice
Joel Rush
Henry Smith
James Smith
Peter Shogger
*Jas C. Seeley
*Ashley Torgusson
Torgus Torgusson
John Thornton
*Joseph Trigg
◊Reuben Wilsey
Asa Ward

Company "F."

Organized August 15, 1862 - From Waseca and Houston Counties.

Captain George T. White, Commissioned September 15, 1862.
*2nd Lieut. Isaac Hamlin, September 15, 1862.
3rd Serg't Lorenzo Curry, September 15, 1862.
5th Serg't Francis S. Brown, September 15, 1862.
2nd Corporal Chas. A. Forrester, September 15, 1862.
5th Corporal Marshal A. Francis, September 15, 1862.
7th Corporal John A. Wheeler, September 15, 1862.
8th Corporal Amos E. Glamiel, September 15, 1862.

Musician
*Simeon S. Goodrich

Wagoner
James R. Whitman

Privates

Wm Beevins
W. B. Blivins
Edw Brossord
Neils Burgerson
And Buchan
*Job A. Canfield
◊Chas Chaddwick
Joseph D. Cox
Theodore Esch
Thos Eldridge
Simeon Wait
Michael Faugle
Jas Gallagher
Sam Gleason
Chas S. Grover
*Silas M. Grover

Knut Hanson
Christian Hatesaul
John Howe
Chas W. Johnston
*Jas Johnson
*Hiram A. Jones
Levi O. Leonard
Dan McDaniels
Andrew Now
Sam Preston
John S. Rice
Henry Ruff
Geo F. Shumway
W. W. Taylor
P. J. D. Wood

Company "G."

On detached service.

Ninth Regiment
Company "H."

Organized August 21, 1862 - From Carver County.

This Company was attached to the 7th Regiment until the Expedition reached Camp Hayes, and Co. D of the 7th joined the Regiment, and then attached to the 10th Regiment until the Expedition reached Fort Abercrombie on its return.

Captain Wm. R. Baxter, Commissioned September 1, 1862.
1st Lieut. Joseph Weinemann, August 14, 1862.
2nd Lieut. Ole Paulson, September 1, 1862.
1st Serg't Allen W. Tiffany, Appointed August 22, 1862.
2nd Serg't George Groetsch, August 22, 1862.

3rd Serg't Andrew Mattson, August 22, 1862.
4th Serg't John M. Foreman, December 7, 1862.
5th Serg't A. G. Anderson, January 1, 1863.
1st Corporal Erastus A. Eddy, August 22, 1862.
2nd Corporal Henry Belz, August 22, 1862.
3rd Corporal M. Berfield, December 7, 1862.
4th Corporal Nelz Olsen, August 22, 1862.
5th Corporal George Raitz, August 22, 1862.
6th Corporal John Carlson, December 7, 1862.
7th Corporal Charles Souter, December 7, 1862.
8th Corporal John Sunden, August 1, 1863.

Musicians

Wm. Stanley Ruse   Peter Dingman

Wagoner   **Bugler**
John Stack   John Hebeisen

Privates

August Arndt
John Arndt
Gottleib Arndt
Thos Armitage
John E. Allen
Burn Aslackson
John Brader
Orson E. Barber
Magnus Bengtson
Lewis Bangson
Andrew Braf
John Blake
Orlando F. Bryant
Joseph Berry
Gustaf Carlson
Peter Carlson
John Denin
Carl Denin
Henry Etzell
And P. Erickson
Xaver Freischle
Thos E. Grove
Benj Guttridge
Geo C. Gay
John R. Goodeno
John Goetz
Peter Halt
John Hanson
G. Hammarberg
G. K. Ives
And Johnson
Jonas Johnson
Nils Johnson
John L. Johnson
Alfred Johnson
Taylor Johnson
John A. Johnson
Jacob Kirsch
Ludwig Klos
Henry Kahle
John Larson
And Larson
Jasper Livingston
Fred Lindquist
Henry Lindert
Theodore Mayres
Allen H. Miller
Ole Olson
David Parks
Pader Paderson
August Peterson
Silas W. Pettijohn
Jacob Pericle
Jesse M. Pericle
John Paluson
Gottleib Plocher
Chas Royle
John Roth
Martin Schaler
And Swanson
Elias Swanson
Fred Souter
Johann Stor
Berger Thurstonson
Ole Wilson
Jas Wilson
Milchoir Wahle
Andre Wallace
Geo Winter

Company "H."

Organized September 13, 1862 - From Rice, Ramsey and Dakota Counties.

Captain Michael H. Sullivan, Commissioned September 13, 1862.
1st Lieut. Dennis Cavenaugh, September 13.
2nd Lieut. Dennis F. McCarty, September 13.
1st Serg't Michael Jeffers, Appointed September 13, 1862.
2nd Serg't Patrick Reeting, September 13, 1862.
*3rd Serg't James O'Brien, September 13, 1862.
4th Serg't Patrick Byrne, September 13, 1862.
5th Serg't Andrew Devereaux, September 13, 1862.
1st Corporal James O'Neil, September 13, 1862.
*2nd Corporal Geo. W. Lightcap, September 13, 1862.
3rd Corporal John Wall, September 13, 1862.
4th Corporal Jeremiah D. Sullivan, September 13, 1862.
*5th Corporal Robert Hunt, September 13, 1862.
6th Corporal James Considine, September 13, 1862.
7th Corporal James Conway, September 13, 1862.
8th Corporal Thomas Kennedy, September 13, 1862.

Musicians

*Clover G. Irvine   *James Kating

Wagoner

Martin Kilroy

Privates

John Buckley	Jas McBride
Chris Byrne	Patrick McAndrew
Patrick Cudmore	Hugh McNeil
Jas Carroll	Patrick McKenna
John Collins	Walter McNallan
Patrick Cronin	John Mulgrew
Patrick Conlin	Thos Murphy
Thos P. Conaughty	Martin Noon
Patrick Condon	*Dan O'Brien
John Callaghan	*John O'Brien
Edw A. Cramsie	Patrick O'Brien
*Bart Costello	Thos O'Maley
Sylvester Dreger	Aman Olson
Chrisopher Dardis	Jas Perkins
Xavier Duna	*Prudeunt Quereut
*Michael Finerty	M. R. Pendegrast
Edward Fox	Michael Roach
Michael W. Henry	John Robbeauge
Miles Henry	Thos Ryan
Albert A. Harper	*Peter Robbeault
Patrick Harris	Patrick J. Smith
Michael Hanley	Edw Sullivan
Nicholas Idoux	David Tierney
John Kelley	Jacob Tope
Hamilton Logue	*John Whalan
Elezear Laclare	—
John Leo	Absent without leave.
Antoine Laduche	Enos Pete
*Thos McManus	Hugh Crawford
Jas McLaughlin	

Company "I."

On detached service - not on Expedition.

Company "K."

Organized August 13, 1862 - From Hennepin and Ramsey Counties.

Captain Michael J. O'Connor,
  Commissioned September 27, 1862.
1st Lieut. Wm. Burns, September 6, 1862.
2nd Lieut. Michael Hoy, September 7, 1862.
1st Serg't James Flannigan, October 1, 1862.
2nd Serg't Wm. Dunn, October 1, 1862.
3rd Serg't Owen Keegan, October 1, 1862.
4th Serg't Cornelius O'Neil, October 1, 1862.
5th Serg't Hugh A. Cox, January 26, 1863.
1st Corporal Thos. McCarron, October 1, 1862.
2nd Corporal Thomas O'Here, October 1, 1862.
3rd Corporal Daniel Bracken, October 1, 1862.
4th Corporal George Stewart, October 1, 1862.
5th Corporal David Shaw, October 1, 1862.
6th Corporal Andrew Welsh, October 1, 1862.
7th Corporal Wm. Broderick, October 1, 1862.
8th Corporal John Sheridan, January 26, 1863.
Drummer- Daniel Molan.

Privates

Alfred Brazett
Patrick Burke
And Condron
Patrick Carney
Thos Clifford
Joseph F. Cobb
James Connelly
James Coyle
M. J. Connelly
John Costello
Jas Conlin
Wm Dealy
David Duchlaet
Timothy Daly
Michael Dixon
Patrick Eustis
Richard Fewer
Patrick Gleason
Thos Gafney
Wm Grace
Joseph Gunia
John Gallagher
Thos Harran

Edw Moran
Robt McCue
John McGraun
Edw Martin
Jas Manning
Patrick Maloney
Jas Manahan
Jas McKeon
Hugh McKann
Wm McCool
Jas McCoy
Jas Nash
Edw Nary
Jas O'Gorman
Wm O'Gorman
Michael O'Gorman
Wm O'Bryan
Patrick O'Connor
Dan Page
Patrick Quinn
James Riley
Luke Roche
John Ready

Cornelius Hayes
Jas Hayes
Thos Hawkins
Wm Hoy
Peter W. Haman
Benj Herron
Carr Hennessey
Patrick Kennedy
Peter Kernan
Thos McDonough
Dan Molan
Dan Murphy
Michael Mahon

Patrick Ronan
Patrick Sheehan
Wm Sheehan
Michael Sommers
Edw Serbert
Zion Swift
John Sheridan
Patrick Sullivan
Alex Sance
Edw Siebert
Timothy Wood
Peter Ward
Patrick White

- The previous list from company K, is from a Muster-in-Roll and may not be completely accurate. It does not distinguish those who were on the Expedition and those who were not.

First Regiment Minnesota Mounted Rangers.
Field and Staff.

Colonel Samuel McPhaill, Commissioned December 30, 1862;
    Lt. Col. November 24, 1862.
1st Major John H. Parker, November 25, 1862; Capt. 4th Minnesota Volunteers.
2nd Major Salmon A. Buell, December 17, 1862.
3rd Major Oren T. Hayes, March 10, 1863.
Surgeon Josiah S. Weiser, October 21, 1862.
2nd Assistant James C. Rhodes, November 22, 1862;
    private Co. C., 7th Minnesota Volunteers.
Adjutant Wm. M. Pierce, January 3, 1863.
Quartermaster Duncan R. Kennedy, September 11, 1862;
    went back from Camp Baker.
Commissary Edward D. Cobb, December 19, 1862.
Chaplain Thomas E. Inman, April 30, 1863; Capt. Co. D.,
    4th Minnesota Volunteers.
Sergeant Major Joseph F. Blodgett, Appointed May 14, 1863;
    Q. M. Serg't Co. C.
Veterinary Surgeon Frank D. Chapman, Appointed May 20, 1863;
    private Co. M.
Chief Trumpeter Frederick Meile, Appointed May 20, 1863; bugler Co. K.
Q. M. Sergeant James J. Green, March 5, 1863; private Co. E.
Com. Sergeant Newton Williams, January 1, 1863; private Co. F.
1st Hospital Steward C. I. Farley, acting, June 28, 1863; Sergeant Co. G.
2nd Hospital Steward George W. Murdock, February 25, 1863; private Co. I.
Saddler Sergeant George Parkes, February 23, 1863; private Co. A.

Company "A."

From Hennepin and Houston Counties.

The following record from Regimental Books; it does not distinguish those on the Expedition from those who were not.

Captain Eugene M. Wilson, Commissioned October 8, 1862.

1st Lieut. Ebenezer A. Goodell, October 8, 1862; 2nd Lt. September 12, 1862.

2nd Lieut. James M. Payne, September 23, 1862.

1st Sergeant Benjamin C. Prentiss.
Q. M. Sergeant Marshal Robinson.
Com. Sergeant John A. Haycraft.
1st Serg't John E. Moore.
2nd Serg't John Wigle.
3rd Serg't Elisha Cowan.
4th Serg't James K. Wilson

5th Serg't Robert M. Sanborn.
1st Corporal Stephen Pratt.
2nd Corporal Charles H. Cleator.
3rd Corporal Paul H. Rosendahl.
4th Corporal Michael J. Bennett.
5th Corporal Archibald McGill.
6th Corporal John McDermott.

Teamsters

David G. White
James Sweeney

Wagoner
Saddler

Benjamin Parker
Frederick E. Vance

Privates

John M. Adams
Alpheus O. Angell
John B. Boseman
John M. Blakeley
Theodore Belden
Bobt Blakeley
John J. Brown
John F. Burt
Richard Clayton
David Cator
Edw Campbell
Wm Campbell
Chas Duprey
Jesse Dores
L. L. Estes
Uriah E. Foster
Richard Fitzsimmons
Arthur Flynn
Giles Farmin
Wilson Gray
Wm Grover
Gilbert Gilbertson
Sam V. Haycraft
Martin Howard
Edw Hughes
John H. Hicks
Patrick Hagerty,
  bugler
Robt H. Jefferson
Ever M. Johnson
Jasper N. Johnson
Wm M. Jolly
Hugh Jones
Thos Kelly
Gustav Knabel
Geo Kile
Jeremiah Leary
Emmanuel Larelly

Ole Larson
Geo W. Lyttle
Nicholas Murphy
Nicholas Muller
Patrick Many
John Marks
Geo H. McGowan
Ole Olson
Patrick O'Connor
Thos Otterman
Geo Perath
Chas Pope
Chas S. Plummer
Geo R. Page
Jas Parker
Isaac N. Russell
Isaac N. Russell jr
Fred M. Raymond
Wm E. Roth
Harrison Rhoades
Royal W. Smith
Jas Scott
Henry Stuteville
Matthew Sullivan
John Sewald
Albert Simon
Peter Stearns
Geo D. Ticknor
And L. Tennison
Benj Wallace
Isaiah W. Watkins
Jas E. White
Michael Whitt
Jabez M. Whitney
Chas Wheatan
Geo D. Windship
Geo H. Winants
Michael Wolf

Company "B."

From Nicollett County.

Captain Horace Austin, Commissioned September 23, 1862.
1st Lieut. Theodore E. Potter, October 11, 1862.
2nd Lieut. Thomas F. West, October 14, 1862.
1st Sergeant L. J. Patch, Appointed October 29, 1862.
Q. M. Sergeant Wm. S. Marston, October 29, 1862.
*Com. Sergeant Henry J. Neal, October 29, 1862.
1st Serg't Wm. H. Hazzard, October 29, 1862.
3rd Serg't Myron W. Smith, October 29, 1862.
4th Serg't Jud Jones, October 29, 1862.
◊5th Serg't Mark L. Wilds, October 29, 1862.
*1st Corporal David D. McDowell, March, 1863.
2nd Corporal Ezra Bacon, July, 1863.
3rd Corporal Henry H. Dudly, October 29, 1862.
4th Corporal Henry Plowman, October 29, 1862.
5th Corporal Henry Goff, October 29, 1862.
6th Corporal Stone Olson, October 29, 1862.
7th Corporal Simeon Childs, October 29, 1862.

Teamsters

Daniel D. Woolsey

Thomas Hughes

Blacksmith
Henry Borgimire

Farrier
Moirson A. Northrup

Saddler
*James H. Ellison

Wagoner
Henry S. Back

Privates

Wm H. Bayer
Ezra Bacon
Even Bringelson
◊Smith N. Burgess
Wm Clapshaw
Hugh Callender
Barney A. Cooper
Niles Cottingham
Harrison Crandall
John Cunningham
Even M. Davis
Wm A. Dodd
John Farrell
Lawren Foster
Wm M. Fay
Wm B. Haslip, killed.

Geo Mather
*John McDowell
John McGerry
And Moore, killed.
*Horace W. Moore
John Murphy, killed.
Ole Nelson
David R. Nickerson
John O'Sheay
*Eagel Olson
Ole Olson 2nd
Simeon Payer
*Dan Pedoine
Geo W. Rogers
Josiah Rogers
Jacob A. Rose

Keton E. Hatcher
Geo Herber
Geo H. Howland
Agel Hungerford
Hendrick Johnson
*John A. Johnson
Albert Johnson
*Wm H. Jones
Geo M. Keenan
Gulick Knutson
Lewis W. Krassine
Simeon Kyser
Edw Larkin
Jos LaLond jr
John W. Latorelle
*Alex Latorelle
Thos H. Lucas

Wm Ray
*Wayne B. Silliman
Jordon Smith
*Jacob Snell
Francis L. Spencer
Gustaf A. Stark, killed.
H. Stutze, wounded.
Jas Tolan
Phil E. Van Blaricom
Oscar F. Wagoner
Lewis Washburne
*Allen S. Woolsey
◊Elijah Woolsey
*Albert Blanchard
John F. Conant
Francis F. Kennedy

Company "D."

From Stearns County.

Taken from Regimental books.

Captain Oscar Taylor, Commissioned October 22, 1862.
1st Lieut. Ambrose Freeman, killed July 24th near Big Mound.
3rd Lieut. John H. Raymond, October 22, 1862.
1st Sergeant Richard Potter, October 27, 1862.
Q. M. Serg't John R. Clark, October 27, 1862.
Com. Serg't Gilbert S. Mattoon, October 27, 1862.
1st Serg't James C. Wilson, October 27, 1862.
2nd Serg't Matthias Wickley, October 27, 1862.
3rd Serg't Samuel H. Morgan, October 27, 1862.
4th Serg't M. Lauermann, October 27, 1862.
5th Serg't Wm. Carrigan, June 3, 1863.
1st Corporal Wm. Parker, October 27, 1862.
2nd Corporal James R. Tracy, October 27, 1862.
3rd Corporal Franklin C. Darling, October 27, 1862.
4th Corporal Gerhard Leiser, October 27, 1862.
5th Corporal Wilson Hustell, October 27, 1862.
6th Corporal Wm. Sterner, December 3, 1862.
7th Corporal Anton Wartenberg, April 27, 1863.
8th Corporal Geo. W. Danton, June 3, 1863.

Teamsters
Henry L. Glazier

Aaron Fadden

Farrier
Hugh Biggerstaff

Blacksmith
Akey C. Johnson

Saddler
Adoniram Briggs

Wagoner
Samuel Holes

Privates

Jas Angel
Albert G. Barton
Benj S. Brown
Jacob V. Brown
Bartley Blain
Peter Behres
Adam Bunt
Henry Berger
Henry Cook
John Coats
E. K. Chamberlain
Jas Carlisle
John Cossairt
Ole Dahl
Jas F. Dicken
John Eich
Adam Emig
John Fuller
Newton Foster
And Fritz
Nathaniel Getchell
John Grandelmyer
Jesse M. Garlington
Patrick Graham
Geo J. Heinan
Jas Hamilton
Rudolph Huhn
Peter Heintz
Matt Johnson
Anthony Herstiens
Celestien Konig
Wm F. Knowlton
John H. Lavague
Geo N. Lavague

Peter Lawson
Chas W. Lambert
John H. Morgan
Augustus G. Morgan
John M. McAlpine
Fred Marte
John W. Moore
Sam Murray
Robt Murray
Michael Meagher
Jas G. Nugent
Peter Peterson
John Peterson
Nels Peterson
Isaac Peterson
Jerome Rogers
John H. Seymore
Geo W. Spauldin
Thos O. Spauldin
Nicholas Schmit
Wm C. Shafenburg
Jacob Sicely
Joshua Stebbins
John Schafer
August Schultz
Wm Schroeder
Sylvester Thompson
Martin Welsh
Jonathan Woll
Jos S. Wilson
Jas M. Wilson
Ira C. Wade
Henry C. Weaver
Wilfred J. Whitefield

Company "E."

From Nicollet County.

(Remained at Camp Atchison.)

◉Captain E. St. Julian Cox, Commissioned November 5, 1862.
1st Lieut. Patrick S. Gardner, November 5, 1862.
2nd Lieut. Peter A. Lentz, November 5, 1862.
1st Sergeant Darins S. Griffin, Appointed November 24, 1862.
Q. M. Sergeant Sylvester A. George, January 24, 1863.
◉Com. Sergeant Uriah E. Northrup, January 24, 1863.

2nd Serg't Samuel C. McCay, January 24, 1863.
3rd Serg't James Corcoran, January 24, 1863.
4th Serg't Louis F. Auer, April 12, 1863.
5th Serg't Patrick C. Lyons, April 12, 1863.
1st Corporal Anthony Leland, November 24, 1862.
2nd Corporal Dennis L. Maher, December 10, 1862.
3rd Corporal John Murtaugh, January 24, 1863.
4th Corporal Martin L. Maher, January 24, 1863.
5th Corporal Albert Frietag, January 24, 1863.
6th Corporal Richard Pfefferle, January 24, 1863.
7th Corporal Wm. Lehr, April 12, 1863.
8th Corporal Patrick Mullin, April 12, 1863.

Teamster
Wm. Langharst

Blacksmith
Adam Frandle

Saddler
James O'Rielly

Wagoner
🍎John Ledden

Bugler
Silas W. Cornell

Privates

Jacob Bauer
Wm Braats
Wm Burghaff
Jas Cleary
Dan Carsall
Julius Copp
Orloff C. Conway
◊Chasper Cotoff
Jas Caniffe
Even P. Davis
Wm Davis
Ande Delaney
Chas Doran
Michael Downs
Patrick Doyle
Jas Gegan
John Howerwas
Jas Hinds
Fred Heinze
John Jennoir
Wm Kahla
Gotleib Kaka
Michael Klasges
Floyd Lawsen
Patrick L. Maher
Jos Martan
Aaron McDonnell
Chas Mische
Cornelius McCarty
Jeremiah McCarty
John McGrath

Owen McGrath
Timothy Murtough
Xavier Oberle
Asliom Olsen
Richard Orr
Henry Otto
Frank Prokosch
Peter Piereth
Jos Reinbold
Geo Sabbath
John Schwickest
Matthias Schumacher
John Schollenberger
Jas Skelly
John Smith
L. W. Smith
Lawrence Smith
Patrick Smith
Wm Smith
Edward Stampfield
Wenzel Tauer
John Thomas
Henry Trautfether
John Turbes
Chas Veigle
Antoine Vogel
◊John Voghtman
Fred Weitig
Stephen Walters
John Weimer
Alex Warsang

Serg't James Grady, Co. L., died July 26, 1863, at Buffalo Lake; wounded in the leg.

Company "F."

◊Captain Joseph Daniels, Commissioned November 20, 1862.
1st Lieut. Asa Barton, June 5, 1863.
2nd Lieut. Charles E. Thurber, November 20, 1862.
1st Sergeant John T. Grimes, Appointed November 20, 1862.
*Q. M. Serg't Stephen Russell, Appointed November 20, 1862.
Com. Serg't Mark Seely, June 5, 1863.
1st Serg't James A. Foote, November 20, 1862.
2nd Serg't Wm. H. Smith, November 20, 1862.
3rd Serg't Lyman E. Postle, November 20, 1862.
4th Serg't Frederic Hyde, November 20, 1862.
5th Serg't Marshal H. Gore, November 20,1862.
1st Corporal Nehemiah P. Pease, November 20, 1862.
2nd Corporal Mason W. Allen, November 20, 1862.
3rd Corporal Simon Moore, November 20, 1862.
4th Corporal Charles H. Crosby, November 20,1862.
5th Corporal David Smith, November 20, 1862.
7th Corporal William Healy, November 20, 1862.
8th Corporal George C. Fisher, November 20, 1862.

Saddler.
*John A. Harris

Blacksmith
Thomas T. Van Wort

Farrier
Benjamin F. McVey

Privates

Galen Amsden
*Wm Ayer
Horace M. Avery
*Geo W. Beebe
Chas H. Brightman
Job Brown
Henry H. Bonney
Andrias Carlson
Jeff Cunningham
Henry Clemons
John Clemetson
Eugene Cadwell
*Alonzo A. Damon
*Geo W. Dunn
James Doonan
*John G. Duff
◊Rinaldo G. Daniels
Geo Daniels
Franklin A. Drew
◊Wm Foster
Birtel Gunderson
Ezra W. Green
John M. Hanson
Ole Halverson
Nelson Hoople
*Abram N. Hoff

James Lowth
*Levi Littlefield
David Luce
*John R. Lilly
John McCole
Geo McGowan
Archibald G. McNee
*Edwin McManus
Wm L. McCullom
*Hiram Miller
Isaac Milner
John Martin
Orin Neal
Olavis Oleson
Ole E. Oleson
Knudt Oleson
Hiram Owen
*Appollos E. Owen
Wm Pelzer
*Wm Pulford
◊Chas W. Palmer
John F. Pearson
Lorenzo D. Porter
*Denarbus B. Rucker
Almos Rexford
Julius H. Ransom

Eliphalet B. Hale
Caleb Hartshorn
Peter Hopper
Ira B. Hyde
*Eli Haviland
Geo P. Harris
*Elbert H. Halsted
John R. Jackson
Freedom Jacobs
Zodok Kohler
◊Harrison Keeney
Henry Lathan

◊Albert Reed
James C. Robinson
*Geo Rappy
*Wm Shadwell
Wm Schultz
Geo H. Smith
*Joseph Steckel
*Preston Tyrrell
Garrett Wall
John E. Wood
Jacob Yeager

Company "G."

Organized November 13, 1862 - From Ramsey and Houston Counties.

Captain Joseph Anderson, Commissioned November 26, 1862;
    2nd Lieut. October 20, 1862.
1st Lieut. Charles E. Leonard, November 20, 1862.
2nd Lieut. Albert R. Field, October 28, 1862.
1st Sergeant Jas. Smith, November 24, 1862.
Q. M. Sergeant Frank C. Griswold, November 24, 1862.
Com. Sergeant Jos. S. Thompson, November 24, 1862.
1st Sergeant William Stout, July 19, 1863.
2nd Serg't Albert B. Lacy, July 19, 1863.
*3rd Serg't Timothy R. Bullis, July 19, 1863.
4th Serg't Gideon Akers, July 19, 1863.
5th Serg't M. F. Dunham, November 24, 1862.
1st Corporal Charles Holmes, November 24, 1862.
2nd Corporal Geo W. Truax, November 24, 1862.
3rd Corporal Wm. Behmer, January 21, 1863.
4th Corporal Edward Neafsey, November 24, 1862.
5th Corporal Henry W. King, November 24, 1862.
6th Corporal Frederic Patoile, November 24, 1862.
*7th Corporal John S. Harrison, July 10, 1863.
8th Corporal Chalon A. Earle, November 24, 1862.

Blacksmith
George Caddy

Farrier
*Michael Heitz.

Saddler
Hayes Mayhew, Jr.

Privates

Woodford Akers	Michael Lanan
Edw Bulger	Geo Lampman
Wm Brown	Louiz L. Marrion
Jas R. Burke	Newell McDonald
John A. Caswelll	Alex Nichol
Sam Collette	Gilbert B. Nafey
◊Abner Comstock	*Peter Patoile
Dennis Daheny	Berzeal D. Paddock
Thos G. Davison	Wm C. Piers
Wm Durkin	Geo Palmer
Jeremiah Dwan	John L. Russell
Geo W. Emeigh	Michael Redington
Jas Ford	Jas Ryan
L. H. Fessenden	*Cassius M. Sprague
*Stephen R. Field	M. R. Swartout
*Isaac G. Freeman	Eugene M. Swartout
Edwin Griffin	C. R. Smith
Jas L. Grant	Treffley St. Aubin
Sam Hutchins	Thos Smith
Fred Haman	Lorenzo Smith
Jas Holleran	Chas M. Stinson
Jas Hiner	◊Wm O. Sherman
Thos Jimson	Henry Thomas
John K. Johnson	Jos Thompson
*Thos Kelly	Edw Tharriat
*Edw Kirky jr	Geo G. Van Alstine
*Sam Layman	Jacob C. Whiting
*Jas Whitmore	Robt M. Weakley
Wm Wooden	Benj F. Youngs
	Wm Young

Company "H."

Organized November, 1862 - From Freeborn County.

Captain George S. Ruble, Commissioned November 22, 1862.
1st Lieut. Charles W. Cromwell, November 22, 1862.
2nd Lieut. Oren D. Brown, November 22, 1862.
1st Sergeant Enoch C. Cowan.
Q. M. Sergeant John E. Tuttle.
Com. Sergeant Thomas Rutledge.
1st Serg't John O' Shea.
2nd Serg't E. Erving Lyle.
3rd Serg't Adolph Waller.
4th Serg't Silas C. Olmsted.
1st Corporal Charles F. Dmarlett.
2nd Corporal Benjamin Strickland.
3rd Corporal Norman I. Andrews.
4th Corporal Sidney J. Smith
5th Corporal Leonard Craig.

6th Corporal Wilson Black.
7th Corporal Antoine Fisher.
8th Corporal Franklin G. Peace.

Farrier
Thos. K. Andrews

Blacksmith
John M. Ames

Privates

Norman I. Andrews
Josiah Bailey
Patrick Bannin
Geo H. Byfield
Carson C. Carr
Vincent K. Carter
Leroy S. Clemens
Jas L. Christie
Timothy Collins
Ambrose Craig
John M. Field
John W. Frazee
Frank D. Hardy
O. S. Hathaway
Chas P. Hanley
F. B. Hetherington
Jas W. Hetherington
Harvey Hill
Matthew Hogan
Jas M. Hollenback
Harrison Hulse
Ira Hultz
John H. Hussey
John Q. Hussey
Jos L. Hoover
Osman B. Jacobs
Ellef Johnson
Peter Johnson
Wm F. Johnson
David E. Jones
Ralph W. Kennedy
Chas H. Kenney
Sam Loomis Jr
Adelbert D. Loveland
Dauphin Mack
Chas A. Mauney
Wm P. Mauney

Chas H. Martin
Chas W. Marks
Chas L. Mason
Fraser McGregor
Jas M. Mills
Arthur McMillen
Chas T. Moses
Jas G. B. Moses
Wm S. Moses
Chas H. Mulliner
John W. Mustaugh
Jos F. Nadean
John Oleson
Stener Oleson
Miron Page
Mortimer W. Perry
Levi F. Preston
Alvin R. Randall
Lewis Sabin
Wm L. Sargen
Michael Sheehan
Asa Smith
Edw H. Taylor
Francis M Terwilleger
Elias S. Terwilleger
David Tubbs
Wm D. Tucker
A. L. Van Osdell
Amherst D. Wait
Jesse Wheeler
Jonas Whitcomb
Wm J. Wilkins
Albert J. Williams
Richard H. Williams
Leroy B. Woodruff
Edmund A. Wright
Sam B. Waterbury

Company "L."

Organized 1862 - From Farribault County.

Captain Peter B. Davy, Commissioned March 26, 1863;
    1st Lieut. December 10, 1862.
1st Lieut.—— Kidder.
2nd Lieut. Orrin G. Davis, December 1, 1862; private November 1, 1862.
Q. M. Sergeant Ezra M. Ellis.
Com. Sergeant Asa S. Warn, July 9, 1863.
1st Serg't Geo. Andrews, December 10, 1862.
2nd Serg't James Grady, wounded; March 28, 1863.
3rd Serg't Samuel K. Lynd, July 9, 1863.
*4th Serg't Edward Eberlin, December 10, 1862.
5th Serg't Abel Sailor, December 10, 1862.
1st Corporal Edmund Duggan.
2nd Corporal Charles Roberts, December 10, 1862.
3rd Corporal Rufus Berger, December 10, 1862.
4th Corporal John Platt, killed July 9, 1863.
5th Corporal Benjamin Franklin, December 10, 1862.
6th Corporal Simeon Pomeroy, December 10, 1862.
7th Corporal Richard Hoback, July 9, 1863.
8th Corporal Henry Sancomb, July 9, 1863.

Saddler

Even Anderson

Wagoner

Lucius Griffin

Blacksmiths

Henry Kamrar

Abraham S. Fry

Privates

Jeff Anderson
*John Brown
Gerard Bakerman
*Mitchell Brassan
Rock Berthiaume
*Alpheus Banning
Hiram Bennett
Jas Banks
Wm Cusick
Jerry Connors
*Sam Carver
Silas Connelly
Geo Cook
Benj Dolbec
Geo Dajsner
*Geo R. Davis
Hubert Dalpie

Henry Johnson
Mihiel Krinka
Jas K. Knapp
Sam Landis
Edward Laramie
Fred Lacroix
Geo Labat
John Magner
James K. Mason
Julius H. Manthie
And More
Jas Magner
John Mendloh
Alex McElroy
Wilford T. Matthews
Jos Osier
Harvey L. Olson

John Emerson
Henry Ellis
Henry C. Ewald
Joseph Ellor
*Geo T. Frandle
*John T. Frandle
Joe Frandle
Geo Foster
*Isaac Fosset
John J. Fosset
Morris Fitzgerold
Edw Grady
*Dan Hazelton
Jas F. Hyland
John Haly
*Ole J. Johnson

Reginald Peterson
Thos W. Pettit
*Jos Robinett, shot by
a Lieut.
Maglair Robideaux
Geo Rude
And Roberts
*Christian Sauer
Lewis A. Stowe
Wm Walter
H. C. J. Weaver
John Weger
Jodn Wisscawer
John Wesley
Dennis Haly

Company "M."

From Chisago and Mower Counties.

1st Lieut. Daniel B. Johnson, December 30, 1862; 2nd Lt. October 8, 1862.
2nd Lieut. John C. Hanley, December 30, 1862, from private.
1st Sergeant Wm. B. Spencer, December 30, 1862.
*Q. M. Serg't George S. Frost, December 30, 1862.
◊Com. Serg't Geo. V. B. Williams, December 30,1862.
1st Serg't Ira Hakes, December 20, 1862.
2nd Serg't Calvin C. Warner, December 20, 1862,
3rd Serg't Wm. Starkey, December 20, 1862.
4th Serg't Joseph F. Smith, December 20, 1862.
*5th Serg't Leonard P. Wilkes, June 5, 1863.
2nd Corporal George Wood, December 30, 1862.
3rd Corporal Wm. Wright, December 30, 1862.
4th Corporal Robert W. Cowan, December 30,1862.
5th Corporal Asa Pettis, December 30, 1862.
6th Corporal Augustus M. Rice, December 30, 1862.
7th Corporal Samuel H. Britts, June 5, 1863.
8th Corporal Samuel H. Starkweather, do.

Farrier
Wm. Harlington

Blacksmith
John Bonjour

Saddler
Jay H. Hhelps

Wagoner
*Robert Lauderdale

Teamster
Edwin G. Benton

Privates

Jas Bodine
Fred Bagge
Fred A. Bardwell
John A. Burch
David A. S. Butts
*Chas Bishop
John Bontsier
Louis Boutseitt
Joseph Bellanger
Henry C. Cornell
Lewis Conner
Hiram Culver
*Geo Dowling
Henry Disher
John Ferrin
Gunder O. Gunderson
Mart O. Gunderson
Simeon Gifford
Richard Huntley
Henry K. Hill
Mortimer Hallett
Solomon Hallett
Dan Hoy
John N. Johnson
*Lewis Johns
Jos Kellen
Wm Kapham
*Caleb Lewis
Peter Leonard
Clement Lovely
Edw Lauderdale

Antoine LaMort
Barnard LaBat
*Warren Marks
Jos McLeod
John A. Manley
James M'Carney
Geo R. Nicholl
Hall H. Orcutt
John H. Orcutt
Sheldin R. Orcutt
Jas Orcutt
*Xavier Paul
Jonathan P. Reeves
*Chas H. Ruddy
Varnos Robinet
Edw C. Starkey
Nehemiah Thomas
Lewis Williams
Wm Wehmyer
Oliver Wilcox
Doctor J. Wilkes
*John Widmer
Lucius Woodworth
Jerome R. Young
John I. Warren
Peter Langeler
Battische Gervais
Simon Elcott

Third Minnesota Battery.

Commissioned and Non-Commissioned Officers.

(Mostly organized from other Regiments. The Company and Regiment of each man are added to his name.)

Captain John Jones, Commissioned February 25, 1863;
    was an Ordnance Sergeant.
1st Lieut. John C. Whipple, Commissioned February 19, 1863.
1st Lieut. Horace H. Western, May 19, 1863.
2nd Lieut. Don A. Daniels, February 2, 1863.
2nd Lieut. Gad Merrill Dwelle, February 28, 1863.
1st Sergeant Harlow McIntyre, Appointed May 19, 1863.

Q. M. Sergeant George F. Brockett, Company F., 9th Regiment,
Appointed June 15, 1863.
1st Sergeant Joseph T. Hammond, Company C., 9th Regiment,
Appointed May 19, 1863.
2nd Sergeant Melvin H. Bromley, Company I., 6th Regiment,
Appointed May 19, 1863.
3rd Sergeant John Hammond, Company B., 7th Regiment,
Appointed May 19,1863.
4th Sergeant George W. DeGroat, Company E., 7th Regiment,
Appointed June 15, 1863.
5th Sergeant Orrin Nason, Company K., 7th Regiment,
Appointed June 15, 1863.
6th Sergeant William G. Allen, Company G., 7th Regiment,
Appointed June 15, 1863.
1st Corporal Dion Swift, Company K., 10th Regiment,
Appointed May 19, 1863.
2nd Corporal Erasmus D. Easton, Appointed May 19, 1863.
3rd Corporal Albert C. Sherman, Appointed May 19, 1863.
4th Corporal Thomas Kelly, Company A., 10th Regiment,
Appointed June 15, 1863.
5th Corporal George S. Cyphers, Company B., 9th Regiment,
Appointed May 19,1863.
6th Corporal Reuben W. Russ, Company B., 8th Regiment,
Appointed June 15, 1863.
7th Corporal Henry Willyard, Company B., 10th Regiment,
Appointed June 15, 1863.
9th Corporal August Harfeldt, Company E., 6th Regiment,
Appointed June 15, 1863.
10th Corporal John McDonnell, Company A., 8th Regiment,
Appointed June 15, 1863.
11th Corporal Francis Sutton, Company B., 9th Regiment,
Appointed June 15, 1863.
12th Corporal Charles Lamby, Company I., 8th Regiment,
Appointed June 15, 1863.
1st Artilleryman Frederic W. Shoultz, Company K., 6th Regiment,
Appointed June 15, 1863.
2nd Artilleryman Lorenzo G. Hamilton, Company F., 7th Regiment,
Appointed June 15, 1863.
1st Musician John R. Goff, Company C., 7th Regiment,
Appointed June 1, 1863.
2nd Musician George O. Jenkins, Company K., 9th Regiment,
Appointed June 24, 1863.
Wagoner Patrick McBride, Company A., 9th Regiment,
Appointed June 26, 1863.

Privates	Company	Regiment
Andrew Killpatrick	A	6th
Hans Olson	A	6th
John Wright	A	6th
Alexander Wood	B	6th
Edwin Cooley	B	6th
George Forbes	B	6th
Erwin G. Fish	C	6th
John Johnson	C	6th
Peter J. Nordeen	C	6th
Wilbur B. Green	D	6th
Thomas P. James	D	6th
Wm. H. H. Williams	D	6th
William A. Hill	E	6th
John H. Meyer	E	6th
John S. Hobart	F	6th
Baker N. Bunch	F	6th
William Dames	G	6th
William A. Hobbs	G	6th
Henry M. Mixter	H	6th
Robert Pett	H	6th
Michael H. Staats	H	6th
Michael Casey	I	6th
David W. Wiggin	K	6th
Calvin Daniels	A	7th
Joseph Ford	A	7th
Wm. J. Wemple	A	7th
Hiram W. W. Bell	B	7th
Jacob Decoudres	B	7th
Oscar Googins	B	7th
George W. Raymond	B	7th
Gilbert Hayford	C	7th
Peter Lanners	C	7th
Robert A. Morrison	C	7th
Eli C. Reynolds	C	7th
Charles E. Barrett	E	7th
Christian Pfraemmer	E	7th
James Eaton	F	7th
Frank C. Mowry	F	7th
Arthur W. DeLaney	H	7th
Julius Frost	I	7th
John Hart	I	7th
Wm. H. Slosson	I	7th
James F. Jones	A	8th
Orient Pond	B	8th
Orange L. Barber	C	8th
Phillip Fromley	C	8th
George Tourtelotte	E	8th

Privates	Company	Regiment
Wm. Morrell	F	8th
John Tompkins	F	8th
Daniel Bloxham	F	8th
Franz Schimp	I	8th
George W. Hall	A	9th
John Zimm	A	9th
Adial Wilcox	C	9th
Thomas Dalen	D	9th
William Shorder	D	9th
Ernest Weikman	D	9th
Morrison M. Burgess	E	9th
James W. Hoozer	E	9th
Alfred Meservey	E	9th
Henry C. Reev	E	9th
Gillett Beecker	F	9th
Addison Hall	F	9th
James H. Marlett	F	9th
Peter Nemirs	K	9th
Joseph R. Rods	K	9th
Jeremiah Elliot	A	10th
Marcus Ware	A	10th
Isaac Johnson	B	10th
Edward Morris	B	10th
Thomas Wiley	B	10th
Irad M. Fuller	C	10th
Henry Snyder	C	10th
George Shakspeare	D	10th
Jossph Rufford	E	10th
Patrick Fausty	E	10th
Jacob Newkirk	F	10th
Camel S. Miles	G	10th
Henry A. Lumph	G	10th
Ferdinand Storback	G	10th
Charles C. Browne	H	10th
Hiram J. Dibble	H	10th
Chandler C. Fleming	K	10th
Michael More	K	10th
George Graves	K	10th
John Killala		
Thomas H. Dring		Alvin B. Taunt
Frederic Goodrich		Samuel W. White
Wm. J. Hutton		George L. Kenyon
Andrew S. Morrow		Lewis Lebert
H. M. Montgomery		Henry LaFlesh
Matthew Steel		Haeftan A. Eckholdt

* Stayed at Camp Atchison.

◊ Was sent to Fort Abercrombie, from Camp McLaren or Camp Hayes.

 Went to Missouri River, while Company stayed at Camp Atchison.

List of troops from:

Arthur M. Daniels, <u>A Journal of Sibley's Indian Expedition During the Summer of 1863 and Record of the Troops Employed/By a Soldier in Company "H," 6th Regiment</u> (Minneapolis, MN: James D. Thueson, 1980).

ABOUT THE AUTHOR

Susan Mary Kudelka's love for history comes both from her Grandfather Earl and her Father Roger. Growing up in Forman, North Dakota, Susan has spent her life traveling across North Dakota visiting every type of historical site and museum. This fascination in learning more about history resulted in a job at the Sargent County Museum. She started out painting the museum's totem pole and went on to help design exhibits for two additions to the museum. Susan attended Dickinson State University for a year and graduated from Minnesota State University in Moorhead in May 2002 with a degree in history. Susan's next project will be working for McCleery & Sons Publishing conducting research for a new book on the history of Sargent County.

ACKNOWLEDGMENT

I would like to thank professor Steven Hoffbeck from Minnesota State University in Moorhead, for his help and encouragement during my years at MSUM. It was during his Senior Seminar class on the American West that I first wrote about the Sibley Expedition.

To order additional copies of
MARCH ON THE DAKOTA'S
please complete the following.

$14.95 EACH
***(plus $3.95 shipping & handling for first book,
add $2.00 for each additional book ordered.***

*Shipping and Handling costs for larger quantites
available upon request.*

Please send me _____ additional books at $14.95 + shipping &
handling

Bill my: ❏ VISA ❏ MasterCard   Expires _____

Card # _____

Signature _____

Daytime Phone Number _____

For credit card orders call 1-888-568-6329
TO ORDER ON-LINE VISIT: www.jmcompanies.com
OR SEND THIS ORDER FORM TO:
McCleery & Sons Publishing
PO Box 248
Gwinner, ND 58040-0248

I am enclosing $_____   ❏ Check ❏ Money Order
Payable in US funds. No cash accepted.

SHIP TO:
Name_____

Mailing Address _____

City _____

State/Zip _____

Orders by check allow longer delivery time.
Money order and credit card orders will be shipped within 48 hours.
This offer is subject to change without notice.

NEW RELEASES

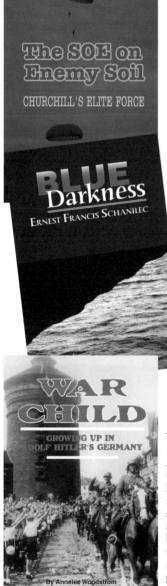

The SOE on Enemy Soil
Churchill's Elite Force
British Prime Minister Winston Churchill's plan for liberating Europe from the Nazis during the darkest days of the Second World War was ambitious: provide a few men and women, most of them barely out of their teens, with training in subversion and hand-to-hand combat, load them down with the latest in sophisticated explosives, drop them by parachute into the occupied countries, then sit back and wait for them to "Set Europe Ablaze." No story been told with more honesty and humor than Sergeant Fallick tells his tale of service. The training, the fear, the tragic failures, the clandestine romances, and the soldiers' high jinks are all here, warmly told from the point of view of "one bloke" who experienced it all and lived to tell about it.
Written by R.A. Fallick. (282 pgs.)
$16.95 each in a 6x9" paperback.

Blue Darkness
This tale of warm relationships and chilling murders takes place in the lake country of central Minnesota. Normal activities in the small town of New Dresen are disrupted when local resident, ex-CIA agent Maynard Cushing, is murdered. His killer, Robert Ranforth also an ex-CIA agent, had been living anonymously in the community for several years. Earlier in his career, Cushing was instrumental during the investigation and subsequent arrest of Ranforth by the FBI for espionage. Ranforth vanished before the trial began. Tom Hastings, a neighbor and friend of the victim, becomes a threat to the anonymous ex-agent. Stalked and attached at his country home, he employs tools and people, including neighbors, a deputy sheriff and Allan Burnside of the FBI, to mount a defense and help solve crimes.
Written by Ernest Francis Schanilec. (276 pgs.)
$16.95 each in a 6x9" paperback.

War Child
Growing Up in Adolf Hitler's Germany
Annelee Woodstrom was twenty years old when she immigrated to America in 1947. These kind people in America wanted to hear about Adolf Hitler, the man who was despised everywhere in the world. During her adolescene, constant propaganda and strictly enforced censorship influenced her thinking. As a young adult, the bombings and all the consequential suffering caused by World War II affected Annelee deeply. How could Annelee tell them that as a child, during 1935, she wanted nothing more than to be a member of Adolf Hitler's Jung Maidens' organization? Written by Annelee Woodstrom (252 pgs.)
$16.95 each in a 6x9" paperback.

Grandmother Alice
Memoirs from the Home Front Before Civil War into 1930's
Alice Crain Hawkins could be called the 'Grandma Moses of Literature'. Her stories, published for the first time, were written while an invalid during the last years of her life. These journal entries from the late 1920's and early 30's gives us a fresh, novel and unique understanding of the lives of those who lived in the upper part of South Carolina during the state's growing years. Alice and her ancestors experiences are filled with understanding - they are provacative and profound. Written by Reese Hawkins (178 pgs.) $16.95 each in a 6x9" paperback.

I Took The Easy Way Out
Life Lessons on Hidden Handicaps
Twenty-five years ago, Tom Day was managing a growing business - holding his own on the golf course and tennis court. He was living in the fast lane. For the past 25 years, Tom has spent his days in a wheelchair with a spinal cord injury. Attendants serve his every need. What happened to Tom? We get an honest account of the choices Tom made in his life. It's a courageous story of reckoning, redemption and peace. Written by Thomas J. Day. (200 pgs.) $19.95 each in a 6x9" paperback.

Tales & Memories of Western North Dakota
Prairie Tales & True Stories of 20th Century Rural Life
This manuscript has been inspired with Steve's antidotes, bits of wisdom and jokes (sometimes ethnic, to reflect the melting pot that was and is North Dakota; and from most unknown sources). A story about how to live life with humor, courage and grace along with personal hardships, tragedies and triumphs. Written by Steve Taylor. (174 pgs.) $14.95 each in a 6x9" paperback.

9/11 and Meditation - *America's Handbook*
All Americans have been deeply affected by the terrorist events of and following 9-11-01 in our country. David Thorson submits that meditation is a potentially powerful intervention to ameliorate the frightening effects of such divisive and devastating acts of terror. This book features a lifetime of harrowing life events amidst intense pychological and social polarization, calamity and chaos; overcome in part by practicing the age-old art of meditation. Written by David Thorson. (110 pgs.) $9.95 each in a 4-1/8 x 7-1/4" paperback.

Eat, Drink & Remarry
The poetry in this book is taken from different experiences in Lynne's life and from different geographical and different emotional places.
Every poem is an inspiration from someone or a direct event from their life...or from hers. Every victory and every mistake - young or old. They slowly shape and mold you into the unique person you are. Celebrate them as rough times that you were strong enough to endure. By sharing them with others, there will always be one person who will learn from them. Written by Lynne D. Richard Larson (86 pgs.)
$12.95 each in a 5x8" paperback.

Phil Lempert's HEALTHY, WEALTHY, & WISE
The Shoppers Guide for Today's Supermarket

This is the must-have tool for getting the most for your money in every aisle. With this valuable advice you will never see (or shop) the supermarket the same way again. You will learn how to: save at least $1,000 a year on your groceries, guarantee satisfaction on every shopping trip, get the most out of coupons or rebates, avoid marketing gimmicks, create the ultimate shopping list, read and understand the new food labels, choose the best supermarkets for you and your family. Written by Phil Lempert. (198 pgs.)
$9.95 each in a 6x9" paperback.

Miracles of COURAGE
The Larry W. Marsh Story

This story is for anyone looking for simple formulas for over-coming insurmountable obstacles. At age 18, Larry lost both legs in a traffic accident and learned to walk again on un-tested prothesis. No obstacle was too big for him - putting himself through college - to teaching a group of children that frustrated the whole educational system - to developing a nationally recognized educational program to help these children succeed. Written by Linda Marsh. (134 pgs.)
$12.95 each in a 6x9" paperback.

The Garlic Cure

Learn about natural breakthroughs to outwit: Allergies, Arthritis, Cancer, Candida Albicans, Colds, Flu and Sore Throat, Environmental and Body Toxins, Fatigue, High Cholesterol, High Blood Pressure and Homocysteine and Sinus Headaches. The most comprehensive, factual and brightly written health book on garlic of all times. INCLUDES: 139 GOURMET GARLIC RECIPES! Written by James F. Scheer, Lynn Allison and Charlie Fox. (240 pgs.)
$14.95 each in a 6x9" paperback.

For Your Love

Janelle, a spoiled socialite, has beauty and breeding to attract any mate she desires. She falls for Jared, an accomplished man who has had many lovers, but no real love. Their hesitant romance follows Jared and Janelle across the ocean to exciting and wild locations. Join in a romance and adventure set in the mid-1800's in America's grand and proud Southland.
Written by Gunta Stegura. (358 pgs.)
$16.95 each in a 6x9" paperback.

From Graystone to Tombstone
Memories of My Father Engolf Snortland 1908-1976

This haunting memoir will keep you riveted with true accounts of a brutal penitentiary to a man-hunt in the unlikely little town of Tolna, North Dakota. At the same time the reader will emerge from the book with a towering respect for the author, a man who endured pain, grief and needless guilt -- but who learned the art of forgiving and writes in the spirit of hope. Written by Roger Snortland. (178 pgs.)
$16.95 each in a 6x9" paperback.

Blessed Are The Peacemakers
Civil War in the Ozarks

A rousing tale that traces the heroic Rit Gatlin from his enlistment in the Confederate Army in Little Rock to his tragic loss of a leg in a Kentucky battle, to his return in the Ozarks. He becomes engaged in guerilla warfare with raiders who follow no flag but their own. Rit finds himself involved with a Cherokee warrior, slaves and romance in a land ravaged by war.
Written by Joe W. Smith (444 pgs.)
$19.95 each in a 6 x 9 paperback

Pycnogenol®

Pycnogenol® for Superior Health presents exciting new evidence about nature's most powerful antioxidant. Pycnogenol® improves your total health, reduces risk of many diseases, safeguards your arteries, veins and entire circulation system. It protects your skin - giving it a healthier, smoother younger glow. Pycnogenol® also boosts your immune system. Read about it's many other beneficial effects. Written by Richard A. Passwater, Ph.D. (122 pgs.)
$5.95 each in a 4-1/8 x 6-7/8" paperback.

Remembering Louis L'Amour

Reese Hawkins was a close friend of Louis L'Amour, one of the fastest selling writers of all time. Now Hawkins shares this friendship with L'Amour's legion of fans. Sit with Reese in L'Amour's study where characters were born and stories came to life. Travel with Louis and Reese in the 16 photo pages in this memoir. Learn about L'Amour's lifelong quest for knowledge and his philosophy of life. Written by Reese Hawkins and his daughter Meredith Hawkins Wallin. (178 pgs.)
$16.95 each in a 5-1/2x8" paperback.

Outward Anxiety - Inner Calm

Steve Crociata is known to many as the Optician to the Stars. He was diagnosed with a baffling form of cancer. The author has processed experiences in ways which uniquely benefit today's readers. We learn valuable lessons on how to cope with distress, how to marvel at God, and how to win at the game of life.
Written by Steve Crociata (334 pgs.)
$19.95 each in a 6 x 9 paperback

Seasons With Our Lord

Original seasonal and special event poems written from the heart. Feel the mood with the tranquil color photos facing each poem. A great coffee table book or gift idea. Written by Cheryl Lebahn Hegvik. (68 pgs.) $24.95 each in a 11x8-1/2 paperback.

Bonanza Belle

In 1908, Carrie Amundson left her home to become employed on a bonanza farm. Carrie married and moved to town. One tragedy after the other befell her and altered her life considerably and she found herself back on the farm where her family lived the toiled during the Great Depression. Carrie was witness to many life-changing events happenings. She changed from a carefree girl to a woman of great depth and stamina.

Written by Elaine Ulness Swenson. (344 pgs.)
$15.95 each in a 6x8-1/4" paperback.

Home Front

Read the continuing story of Carrie Amundson, whose life in North Dakota began in *Bonanza Belle*. This is the story of her family, faced with the challenges, sacrifices and hardships of World War II. Everything changed after the Pearl Harbor attack, and ordinary folk all across America, on the home front, pitched in to help in the war effort. Even years after the war's end, the effects of it are still evident in many of the men and women who were called to serve their country. Written by Elaine Ulness Swenson. (304 pgs.)
$15.95 each in a 6x8-1/4" paperback.

First The Dream

This story spans ninety years of Anna's life - from Norway to America - to finding love and losing love. She and her family experience two world wars, flu epidemics, the Great Depression, droughts and other quirks of Mother Nature and the Vietnam War. A secret that Anna has kept is fully revealed at the end of her life.

Written by Elaine Ulness Swenson. (326 pgs.)
$15.95 each in a 6x8-1/4" paperback

Pay Dirt

An absorbing story reveals how a man with the courage to follow his dream found both gold and unexpected adventure and adversity in Interior Alaska, while learning that human nature can be the most unpredictable of all. Written by Otis Hahn & Alice Vollmar. (168 pgs.)
$15.95 each in a 6x9" paperback.

Spirits of Canyon Creek

Sequel to "Pay Dirt"

Hahn has a rich stash of true stories about his gold mining experiences. This is a continued successful collaboration of battles on floodwaters, facing bears and the discovery of gold in the Yukon.

Written by Otis Hahn & Alice Vollmar. (138 pgs.)
$15.95 each in a 6x9" paperback.

Whispers in the Darkness

In this fast paced, well thought out mystery with a twist of romance, Betty Pearson comes to a slow paced, small town. Little did she know she was following a missing link - what the dilapidated former Beardsley Manor she was drawn to, held for her. With twists and turns, the Manor's secrets are unraveled. Written by Shirlee Taylor. (88 pgs.)
$14.95 each in a 6x9" paperback.

Dr. Val Farmer's Honey, I Shrunk The Farm

The first volume in a three part series of Rural Stress Survival Guides discusses the following in seven chapters: Farm Economics; Understanding The Farm Crisis; How To Cope With Hard Times; Families Going Through It Together; Dealing With Debt; Going For Help, Helping Others and Transitions Out of Farming. Written by Val Farmer. (208 pgs.)
$16.95 each in a 6x9" paperback.

Country-fied

Stories with a sense of humor and love for country and small town people who, like the author, grew up country-fied . . . Country-fied people grow up with a unique awareness of their dependence on the land. They live their lives with dignity, hard work, determination and the ability to laugh at themselves. Written by Elaine Babcock. (184 pgs.)
$14.95 each in a 6x9" paperback.

Charlie's Gold and Other Frontier Tales

Kamron's first collection of short stories gives you adventure tales about men and women of the west, made up of cowboys, Indians, and settlers. Written by Kent Kamron. (174 pgs.) $15.95 each in a 6x9" paperback.

A Time For Justice

This second collection of Kamron's short stories takes off where the first volume left off, satisfying the reader's hunger for more tales of the wide prairie. Written by Kent Kamron. (182 pgs.) $16.95 each in a 6x9" paperback.

It Really Happened Here!

Relive the days of farm-to-farm salesmen and hucksters, of ghost ships and locust plagues when you read Ethelyn Pearson's collection of strange but true tales. It captures the spirit of our ancestors in short, easy to read, colorful accounts that will have you yearning for more. Written by Ethelyn Pearson. (168 pgs.)
$24.95 each in an 8-1/2x11" paperback.

(Add $3.95 shipping & handling for first book, add $2.00 for each additional book ordered.)